THE
Charlie Chan
MYSTERY MOVIE GUIDE

LUKE FREEMAN

PARASOLO BOOKS

ISBN-10: 0-9925619-0-6
ISBN-13: 978-0-9925619-0-1

THE CHARLIE CHAN MYSTERY MOVIE GUIDE

TABLE OF

ACT I:

WARNER OLAND AS CHARLIE CHAN
AT FOX FILMS / TWENTIETH CENTURY-FOX

CONTENTS

ACT II:

CHARLIE CHAN WITH **SIDNEY TOLER** AT TWENTIETH CENTURY-FOX

ACT I

WARNER OLAND

CHARLIE CHAN IN LONDON (1934)

"World is large. Me lowly Chinaman"
- Charlie Chan

Warner Oland (Charlie Chan), **Drue Leyton** (Pamela Gray), **Raymond Milland** (Neil Howard), **Mona Barrie** (Lady Mary Bristol), **Alan Mowbray** (Geoffrey Richmond), **Murray Kinnell** (Phillips), **Douglas Walton** (Hugh Gray), **Walter Johnston** (Jerry Garton), **E. E. Clive** (Sergeant Thacker), **George Barraud** (Major Jardine), **Madge Bellamy** (Mrs. Fothergill), **David Torrence** (Home Secretary), **John Rogers** (Lake), **Paul England** (Bunny Forthergill), **Elsa Buchanan** (Alice Rooney), **Perry Ivans** (Kemp).

Director: **Eugene Forde**
Screenplay: **Philip MacDonald**
Runtime: 79 mins. Fox Film Corp.

Film 6 in the Charlie Chan *series, and the first not based on a novel by Chan creator Earl Derr Biggers.*

SYNOPSIS: The first *Charlie Chan* film beyond the novels of author Earl Derr Biggers sees our favorite Chinese-Hawaiian Detective in London, where the sister of a man wrongfully convicted of murder and sentenced to death pleads for his assistance. Chan has just 65 hours to uncover the real killer before the innocent man is sent to the gallows.

Humility

A fidgety man in a prison cell anxiously awaits word of his fate. His sister arrives, but with the news that the petition to stay his execution has been rejected. The news momentarily sends the man into a crestfallen, almost trance-like state of defeat, but his sister refuses to lose faith, and somehow her hope keeps him buoyed too. Still utterly convinced of his innocence, her next step, accompanied by her fiancé (who was also the condemned man's defense barrister), is an audience with the Home Secretary. But the Home Secretary, describing himself as "merely a mouthpiece of the state" is not only of no help, but actually aghast when the woman has the nerve to suggest that, in executing her brother, the state will be committing murder; "State? Murder?" he brays, bewildered. "Why I've never...". From the Secretary we learn that the woman and her barrister fiancé have gone down every proper channel and pursued every official avenue in effort to free her brother, but may now have reached the end of the line. "Your brother has been tried and found guilty. The court of appeal sustained the original verdict, and a petition for reprieve has been rejected. The law must take its course".

But there *is* one last hope. Hearing that Charlie Chan, the famous detective of the Honolulu Police, is in town, the condemned man's sister and her fiancé rush to his hotel to plead for his assistance. They arrive to find him already packing for his return trip home to Honolulu, and though he listens to their story and is sympathetic to their cause, he's not really sure how they think that he can help. "World is large, me lowly Chinaman" he says, mystified by the woman's absolute faith in his ability to clear and free her brother, particular in light of the deadline of "65 small hours" with which to work with before the man is hanged. But when a row between the woman and the barrister over the situation results in their breakup, and in her angrily throwing off her engagement ring as she storms away, Chan feels compelled to take on the case.

That evening, Chan visits the country estate where the murder took place, and where the witnesses from the night of the murder (with the real killer hidden among them) have returned for a fox hunting weekend. With no time to waste, this eclectic collection of genteel types are soon to be treated to Chan's seemingly unconventional, but in fact highly rational (and effective), methods of investigation. Chan immediately has the suspects rounded up and gathered in the study, where he declares that one of them is the real killer (as is customary in mystery yarns of this kind, though usually at the climax, when the detective is ready to reveal all, not at the *beginning* of the investigation). After digesting some testimony from each of the witnesses, Chan then proceeds to drag them all along with him on his investigation, outside in the chilly night air, around the estate grounds, and to the scene of the crime: the horse stables. It's there that he begins to go about unraveling the clues, rubbishing the statements his tour party each gave to him moments earlier, and systematically separating the facts from the horse manure within. He takes them (and us) through the procedural method of reconstructing the murder, and though this prim and proper group can gripe and complain all they like about it - "what a lot of childish nonsense", "if you think I'm going though with this tomfoolery...", etc - somehow they all end up complying with Chan's seemingly bizarre requests; playing their designated undignifying parts in Chan's re-enactment of the crime. And there proves to be method in Chan's madness, with the activity of the re-enactment setting off the violently loud braying of the nearby horse, which had been oddly silent on the night of the murder, thus raising the first real shred of doubt regarding the convicted man's guilt. Chan may have been late in being summoned to the stable door, but this horse hasn't necessarily yet bolted!

In the decades since CHARLIE CHAN IN LONDON premiered, much has been made of Chan's polite manner and gentle disposition. How much of it is simply his true nature, how much of it is a put on, and how much of it is a sly dig toward those with whom he's conversing, one isn't always exactly sure, but with Warner Oland portraying the Oriental sleuth, we get the feeling that it's all very much genuine. There's a sincerity about him that shines through with every word he speaks, his famous "thank you, so much" always sounding like real gratitude, whatever he happens to be saying it in response to, and every bit as sincere is the humility he forever displays upon being told that his name and reputation have preceded him (even when it is for the umpteenth time).

Whatever the case, it enables him to get away with murder. Within a few minutes of arriving at the estate, Chan breaks into a woman's bedroom via a climb through the window, scares the living suitcase out of the chambermaid, forces two men into re-enacting a gruesome murder, actually calls one person "the murderer" (listen closely), and in a polite, humble, and smiling way, goes about giving everyone orders. It's here one realizes that Chan's manners could be the velvet glove that covers an iron fist. He talks in aphorisms but is very much forthright; speaking politely while going straight for the jugular. His "excuse please, but..." is usually followed by a remark that would in any other circumstances be inexcusable, and his "contraction please, but..." by an observation that exposes the other person's statement as completely erroneous. Only someone as polite as Charlie Chan could get away with being as rude as Charlie Chan.

It's his obedient nodding and Cheshire cat grinning, referring to himself as "humble" and everybody else as "honorable", that allows this self-described "lowly Chinaman" to rise above his purported subservient station, and stand over and above those who may have otherwise considered him beneath them. True, his profession, and the critical nature of this particular situation, help - "when death enters window, no time for life to go by door" he explains, when awkwardly caught crawling out from under a desk - but no one else could cut though the pompousness and pretentiousness of this country estate in the way he does, or tell a room full of people of higher social standing and rank that one of them is a killer. A real gentle man among purported gentlemen, and by far the most genuinely well-manned of this lot, even amidst the pressure put on him, he won't let other people's reactions, or the mere fact that that a man's life is at stake, goad him into panic, knowing he can only "do humble best". The smartest person in the room, he knows that the stud groom Lake's death is unlikely to be suicide, for the murdered man left a large wad of cash behind, and Chan knows that "man in lowly station does not kill himself when possessing such money"; an observation no one else present could have thought of. But then later watch how he respectfully placates the process-obsessed local detective, Thacker. Sergeant Thacker, who "knows (his) duty", and factiously writes every detail down in his notebook, not because he intends ever to read back over it or draw upon it, but rather because he vaguely hopes that the mere ritual of dimly carrying out the procedure will somehow, in some way, help him. But this is his turf that Chan is impinging upon, and somehow Chan knows how get the Sergeant on side, deferentially, while still saying and doing exactly what he wants to. Richmond, the guests, the staff, the various police and officialdom: Everyone in this film knows their place and minds their manners and follows the correct procedures and goes through the proper channels and adheres to all the dictated protocols and accepted social norms and conventions, except for the most polite one of them all, Charlie Chan, who instead forges his own path.

And yet, there's no arrogance or dishonesty here. For Charlie Chan, humility *isn't* the worst form of conceit, or even the best form of deceit. It's simply what comes honestly and naturally. It's simply Charlie Chan being Charlie Chan.

Much of credit for making this work goes, of course, to Warner Oland. Oland immersed himself in the role, not so much playing Charlie Chan as sort of becoming him. The formal manner, the wise, Confucius-like sayings: these attributes could have felt like extraneous gimmicks bolted on, but instead they feel like something core and fundamental to the character. When Oland delivers one of those famous Chanisms, such as "if you want wild bird to sing, do not put him in cage", he makes them feel like genuine philosophies that the character lives his life by, drawn from a reservoir deep

13

within himself, as opposed to merely, say, a clever line written for the moment by a scriptwriter.

Though neatly plotted and nicely executed, CHARLIE CHAN IN LONDON doesn't quite reach the top echelon of Chan films. For one, it's overly static, stagey and talky, even compared to the films that immediately follow. The identity of the killer is obvious midway though, and when Chan eventually smokes him out, it's with a rather unsophisticated trap: the old "give the murderer an unloaded gun and see if he tries to kill you" trick (though to be fair, back in 1935 it may very well have been known as the *new* "give the murderer an unloaded gun and see if he tries to kill you" trick).

But the plot is strong and the execution charming and compelling and focused, not as slick as some future entries, but not as mechanical or by-the-numbers either, while a good supporting cast of character actors (including Alan Mowbray and E. E. Clive, plus a young Ray Milland) aid in making it all feel real and important and real important. We're made to genuinely care about the condemned man's plight, and about the sister and barrister's love story. The race against time to save Gray from execution, the constant worrying that time is running out, creates a genuine sense of urgency amid the sedate country house setting. Of course, we know that it will all turn out fine in the end, but while the events are in motion we care that it does.

The picture's real asset, though, is Warner Oland, who, front and centre of it all for nearly every minute, is a real delight throughout. If detective story is really only as good as its protagonist, then CHARLIE CHAN IN LONDON at least has one the best in Warner Oland as Charlie Chan.

"To the greatest detective in the world" the liberated Paul Gray toasts at the end of the picture, having been rescued by Chan from a one way trip to the gallows. Of course, Charlie Chan, humble as ever, refutes the grateful man's claim: "No, not very good detective. Just lucky old Chinaman".

BEST MOMENT: [16:13] - Chan arrives at the Richmond house. He knocks on the door. The butler appears and Chan asks to see Pamela Gray. Chan attempts to explain that the matter is "most urgent", but the butler will hear none of it. Blocking Chan's entrance, he curtly tells him that he "must return on the morning", and doesn't even wait for a response before dismissively slamming the door in his face. "Thank you, so much" Chan, still on the outer, replies to no-one.

Finding the standard entry blocked, the conventional path a dead end, a completely undeterred Chan instead just walks around the building and climbs up through Pamela's bedroom window in order to get his desired audience with her. "Excuse, please" he smiles to the horrified chambermaid waiting on Pamela, his offer of "1000 apologies" for his unconventional mode of entry doing naught to placate the shrieking woman. But Pamela, elated to see him, sends the flabbergasted maid away, and Chan explains that he has decided to take on the case.

Getting to work, Pamela and Chan head downstairs, and Pamela asks the butler - the same butler who wouldn't let Chan inside the house but a few moments earlier - to show Chan to the study. "This way please", the butler stiffly directs, to which Chan quietly chuckles, and again replies "Thank you, so much".

IN SHORT: A charming, compelling mystery, benefiting from strong plotting, good casting, and a fine country estate setting.

CHARLIE CHAN IN PARIS (1935)

"Kindness in heart better than gold in bank"
- Charlie Chan

Warner Oland (Charlie Chan), **Keye Luke** (Number One Son Lee), **Mary Brian** (Yvette Lamartine), **Thomas Beck** (Victor Descartes), **Erik Rhodes** (Max Corday), **John Miljan** (Albert Dufresne), **Murray Kinnell** (Henri Latouche), **Minor Watson** (Renard), **John Qualen** (Concierge), **Henry Kolker** (M. Lamartine), **Dorothy Appleby** (Nardi), **Ruth Peterson** (Renee Jacuard), **Perry Ivans** (Bedell).

Director: **Lewis Seiler**
Writers: **Edward T. Lowe** and **Stuart Anthony** (screenplay), **Philip MacDonald** (story)
Runtime: 72 mins. Fox Film Corp.

Film 7 in the Charlie Chan *series, and the first featuring Key Luke as Number One Son Lee.*

SYNOPSIS: Charlie Chan travels to Paris to investigate a bond-forgery scheme.

Kindness

"It is always considered good fortune to give alms upon entry to city" chimes Charlie Chan, as he offers a few coins to a local beggar upon arriving in Paris, but within his first few hours after touching down in the city of light, Chan is nearly hit by a threatening note thrown though his cab window, sees his contact, an Apache dancer, murdered right before his eyes while performing her dance at a nightclub, and then is almost killed himself, narrow avoiding being crushed by a falling cinder block aimed at his skull. "The purpose of your visit is known. If you place the least value upon your LIFE, leave France TONIGHT. This will be your only WARNING" reads his welcome notice, as Chan's philosophy of "See Paris. Then die" starts to look more a possibility by the minute.

Like CHARLIE CHAN IN LONDON, CHARLIE CHAN IN PARIS takes its time - but wastes no time - in the way that it neatly and efficiently paints its character portraits, establishes its setting, and lays out its story. We have, of course, the young lovers in peril: this time the cheery, dapper Victor (played by Thomas Beck), and his fiancé, the equally bright and chipper Yvette (Mary Brian). Victor's father is a director of the bank Yvette's father is the head of, and perhaps Victor will eventually become a director of the bank himself - in about twenty years, but for now, starting at the bottom in his 9-to-5 clerk job is okay by him, as he also gets to enjoy plenty of play ("after (work) my time's my own" he beams). Meanwhile, he and Yvette, clearly in love, plan soon on getting married, going on their honeymoon, and beginning their life together.

By setting up this nice young couple and their future plans, the writers clearly establish what will be in jeopardy when Yvette is discovered standing over banker Albert Dufresne's dead body holding the gun that was used to shoot him, and what will be ruined if Chan can't dispose of Yvette's old love letters to Dufresne, and clear her of his murder.

Yvette, of course, is innocent, but cannot reveal to anyone but the kind and understanding Chan the real reason as to why she was there at Dufresne's apartment - to recover her old love notes to him - at the moment he was killed, placing her in a serious bind. After watching her grilling at the hands of the police, in which she desperately protests her innocence but guardedly offers no answers, Chan quietly approaches her. Standing next to her, he opens a book and pretends to peruse it, his eyes on the pages, but his focus very much on her. "You are engaged to very nice young man. Desire to help, if can" he whispers, as she discreetly slips him the aforementioned recovered letters and tells him to destroy them. Advising her to answer no more questions, "silence big sister to wisdom", he ends with a reassuring smile, and then sets to work; our

17

benevolent hero taking it upon himself to set things straight and make everything right.

The case itself is nicely plotted and presented, sustaining suspense and maintaining interest right from the very moment Chan's plane lands. Arriving in Paris, Chan phones his contact, the dancer Nardi, who tells us nothing more than that she has "really discovered something". Whatever that something is, it's too important to risk talking about over the phone, so they agree to meet after her performance at the *Café Du Singe Bleu* later that evening. Then, moments later, just as he's getting into his cab, Chan receives a threatening message - in the form ominous note hurtled though cab window - telling him that the reason for his visit is known and warning him to leave Paris immediately. But instead, he instructs the driver to "proceed to address given", that being of Victor, where he makes arrangements for an appointment with the president of Victor's bank the next morning. He then goes to the nightclub for his rendezvous with Nardi, only to see her murdered before they can talk. He visits her apartment and finds, hidden in the cuckoo clock, the information she left for him. Then, as he exits her building, he is almost killed himself; nearly crushed by a falling cinderblock dropped by an unknown assailant!

And *then*, the next morning, he visits the Lamartine Bank for his meeting with the head of the bank, where he now finally reveals the full nature of his business in Paris, outlaying the details regarding a series forged bonds that have been issued by the bank, and revealing his orders to investigate the matter.

With this approach, placing Act 1's incidents before the exposition, the film successfully underlines the importance of Chan's mission and the lengths that someone is willing to go to in order to stop him, piquing our curiosity and capturing our interest and attention from the outset, *before* the sit-down explanation where we find out what exactly it's all about. Why is Chan in Paris? Why is he so insistent on making an appointment with the bank president? Who are Chan's enemies and how is it that they seem to be one step ahead of him? What has Nardi uncovered? Why was she murdered? These things we are made to wonder and these things we want to find out.

Aside from making us more interested in the business of the bonds than we otherwise might have been, putting the exposition at the *end* of Act 1, rather than at the beginning, also emphasizes the secret nature of Chan's investigation. From these short, brisk sequences, we can tell immediately that Chan is involved in a case of some kind, that it's important enough to demand caution and close secrecy, and that sinister forces are at play, willing to issue serious threats, and even to kill, over whatever it is that's at stake. We know that Chan's life is in danger, and he knows it to, but we also see, first by the way he steadfastly instructs his driver to "proceed to address given" after receiving the threatening note, and then by the way he shakes off his near-death experience with the cinderblock, that he's fixated on his goal and isn't going to back down.

The case of the forged bonds is tied-in skillfully with the two murders and with Yvette's predicament - the first murder setting the stakes, the second raising them - and the final solution, involving Marcel Xavier, the mysterious crippled war veteran who seems to be everywhere, is very clever. These early Chan films successfully moved from Earl Derr Biggers adaptations to original story ideas without missing a beat; the thematic richness of a novel still present in these original 70-odd minute feature film scripts. There's even time for Chan and the local Police Inspector Renard to engage in a nice philosophical discussion about the case over coffee and donuts at a local cafe. "Perfect case, like perfect donut, has hole" smiles Chan. "Optimist only see donut, pessimist see hole".

Keye Luke makes his debut as the devoted Number One Son Lee in this film. Lee is in Paris for a holiday, but insists on helping out when he learns of the attempt made on his Pop's life: "if somebody's gunning for you, I'm staying". Chan immediately puts his son to work following leads and tailing suspects, and the dedicated Number One Son proves his worth (the scene in which Chan leaves Lee to guard a suspect and Lee learns from his prisoner that his father is walking into a trap is particularly well played by Luke).

The film's chic photography makes wonderful use of dark and light: from early on, when Chan, with flashlight in hand, searches in the still darkness of Nardi's apartment in the dead of night, to the finale, where Chan and Victor edge their way though the sewers and underground tunnels of Paris to uncover makeshift lab and printing press where the phony bonds were being made; the two intruders really make to feel like unwelcome visitors in dangerous territory. One would also be remiss not to mention the fast, furious, almost violent Apache dance performed by Nardi and her dance partner at the *Café Du Singe Bleu* earlier; a aromatic, mesmerizing, dance of death that literally ends that way when Nardi is killed by a knife thrown by the mysterious Xavier. Overall CHARLIE CHAN IN PARIS is a more cinematic, more artistic, more stylish, more striking, and more satisfying work than CHARLIE CHAN IN LONDON, and whether it's in comforting the dying Nardi with a soft gesture of his hand, or reassuring the distressed Yvette with a heartening smile, Chan's simple, unspoken kindness is the light that shines through the darkness.

When the mysteries of the forged bonds and the murders of Nardi and Dufresne are solved, Chan still has one more donut hole to fill: A reason for Yvette being in the murdered Dufresne's apartment. To explain her presence there, he claims she was working as his assistant, and that the letters she went there to acquire were in fact important evidence for him. Renard doesn't exactly buy this story, but he knows Chan and he knows Chan's kind heart, and he's willing to go along with him. And after all, this is Paris. "So the age of chivalry isn't dead after all" he smiles knowingly.

BEST MOMENT: [6:12] - The subject of race is very briefly touched upon when Victor introduces Chan to a party of his friends. One of them, the drunken Max Corday, greets Chan with an embarrassing display of condescending Pidgin English, "me very happy know you", "maybe you likee havee little drinkie?" he asks, rather pleased with his impersonation. But his smile collapses when a peeved Chan responds. "Very happy to make acquaintance of charming gentleman" Chan clearly and eloquently retorts, electing to fight prejudice not with more prejudice, but with kindness and a smile, gently, but also very firmly, putting the bigot in his place.

Having turned the knife around, and plunged it straight back into Corday, Chan then twists it just a little, imitating Corday's imitation - "Me no likee drinkie now, perhaps later - but instead of finishing him off, the merciful Chan, mindful of his host, and considering Corday sufficiently chastised, yields, and instead keeps the atmosphere light, to the laughter of all, including Corday.

Whatever the case, the point is well made. When Chan visits Corday at his home the following night, Corday, taking Chan by the arm, remarks "This time I'm not going to ask you to have a 'drinkie', but I want you to have a drink".

IN SHORT: A highly cinematic, artistic, striking, and satisfying work all round. Romantic and aromatic, very chic, and very good. One of a kind.

CHARLIE CHAN IN EGYPT (1935)

"Insignificant molehill sometimes more important that conspicuous mountain"
- Charlie Chan

Warner Oland (Charlie Chan), **Pat Paterson** (Carol Arnold), **Thomas Beck** (Tom Evans), **Frank Conroy** (Prof. Thurston), **Jameson Thomas** (Dr. Anton Racine), **Nigel de Brulier** (Edfu Ahmad), **Rita Hayworth** (Nayda), **James Eagles** (Barry Arnold), **Paul Porcasi** (Fouad Soueida), **Arthur Stone** (Dragoman), **Stepin Fetchit** (Snowshoes), **George Irving** (Prof. Arnold), **John Davidson** (Chemist), **Frank Reicher** (Dr. Jaipur).

Director: **Lewis King**
Screenplay: **Robert Ellis** and **Helen Logan**
Runtime: 72 mins. Fox Film Corp.

Film 8 in the Charlie Chan *series.*

SYNOPSIS: The French Archaeological Society sends Charlie Chan to Egypt, where the newly-uncovered antiquities of an expedition they funded are being stolen and sold to rival museums. Upon arrival, Chan uncovers the expedition leader's murdered body hidden inside a mummy case.

Travels

In CHARLIE CHAN IN LONDON, genteel archetype characters, a country estate setting, and a fox hunting weekend were used as a means of conveying England to us. In CHARLIE CHAN IN PARIS, Gay Paree was depicted via its night life and social life, its restaurants and cafes, and of course, the climatic confrontation in the sewers beneath the city. For CHARLIE CHAN IN EGYPT, however, the filmmakers really stepped it up, using sets and props and mummies tombs and secret chambers and hidden treasures and hieroglyphics to *really* give us Egypt.

And whereas CHARLIE CHAN IN LONDON began with Chan already in the city, and CHARLIE CHAN IN PARIS opened with Chan's plane touching down, CHARLIE CHAN IN EGYPT again goes the extra step, with Chan's rickety plane flight - from which he looks down in awe over the pyramids, the sphinx, and the desert dunes - and then his uncomfortable mule ride - in which he combats the heat and wind and sand and dust – conspiring to really make his journey to the land of the pharaohs feel like a trek into the great unknown: Astonishing from afar, treacherous up close.

Continuing on his travels from the previous film, Chan has journeyed to Egypt on behalf of the French Archaeological Society, who had a contract with a excavation team which stipulated that any artifacts discovered by the team that were not claimed by the Egyptian Government were to become the property of the Society Museum. It turns out, however, that some of the pieces uncovered by the expedition have leaked to rival museums and private collectors, and the Society has sent Chan to Egypt to demand an explanation.

Upon arrival, however, Chan learns that the expedition's leader, Professor Arnold, has been missing, away on another expedition and incommunicado, for over a month. Arnold's partner and brother-in-law Professor Thurston, and his assistant Tom Evans, claim that this long absence without word is no cause for concern, however, Arnold's daughter, Carol, is convinced that something is terribly, terribly wrong.

Adamant that the artifacts said to have turned up in rival museums must be imitations, Thurston and Tom lead Chan to their laboratory to show him the genuine pieces. In the laboratory, they proudly show him their most impressive find, the mummy case of the powerful high priest Ameti, but are shocked when Chan points out that the case has been tampered with. Curious, Chan, Thurston and Tom pry open the case and find, inside, wrapped in white linen with a bullet in his chest, the murdered body of Professor Arnold.

23

It's a superb set up for mystery, and it's a mystery in which Chan finds himself with several problems to solve. Who drugged Carol's cigarettes? Who used the typewriter to type the message claiming to be from Arnold two weeks after Arnold was killed? Who tried to scare Chan and Tom Evans away from the tomb, and just how did they then escape from the tomb if Chan and Tom were blocking the only entrance? And how was the death of Professor Arnold's violin-playing son Barry pulled off, if everyone who might have done it was with Chan at the time of the murder?

In solving these puzzles you can rest assured that there'll be lots of snooping around with flashlights in the dead of night while increasingly ominous music plays in the background, with the feeling that every step forward must made with extreme trepidation and utmost caution permeating though the air. In a terrific sequence we watch as Chan and Tom solve the riddles of Ameti's tomb: first noting the differing hieroglyphics on the walls, then discovering the life and death symbols on the stones, that, when pressed together, open a secret door to a hidden chamber. And then finally, with the use of just a torn bit of paper, establishing that the water in the secret chamber's small pool has a current, and therefore *must* have another side. And so Tom dives in and swims under the wall, where, sure enough, on the other side, the glistening treasure of Ameti awaits. In the chamber Tom also discover other riches, namely the mask that was used to try to scare them off earlier, as well as clothing that belonged to late Professor Arnold; this proving that the Professor *did* discover the treasure and that he *was* killed for it. Of course, at that moment, the same almost happens to Tom, who is shot in the chest, critically injured, and saved from death only by using his flashlight as a shield from the gunman.

The storytelling is clear and solid, the clues and puzzles cleanly disassembled by Chan. Just as the others involved start to question him, and just as it seems that he is no longer a welcome guest, he comes good. First, he demonstrates how the sabotage of Barry's violin was accomplished, the violin rigged with thin glass tube filled with poison gas, that breaks only when a certain sound is played. Then he points out how one of the bullets fired at Tom hit the lens of the flashlight, deducing that the light must have been pointed at the killer at the time of impact, meaning that the unconscious Tom *must* have seen the murderer's face, and will be able to identify them when he wakes up. Unless of course, the shooter can finish him off before he recovers. And with that, a trap is set for our killer.

CHARLIE CHAN IN EGYPT is a mysterious, haunting, riveting concoction, topped off with eerie music, a horror atmosphere, and the usual good casting. Future star Rita Hayworth (biller under real name Rita Cansino) has a small role as the housemaid Naya. Thomas Beck, who had the romantic lead role in CHARLIE CHAN IN PARIS, returns in a similar role, but this character, while still sympathetic, has a slightly harsher side, particularly in his curt treatment of Shepin Fetchit's Snowshoes, who he routinely berates and browbeats. Meanwhile Frank Conroy is suitably suspicious as Thurston, the victim's shady business partner and brother-in-law. Not everyone watching the film today will be enamored with some of the early talkie style of melodrama acting throughout, but Pat Paterson's performance as Carol, the murdered Professor Arnold's emotionally fragile daughter, adds not only a human element to the story, but also a genuine sense of urgency. First desperate to find her father, then in grief over the loss her equally-highly strung brother, then anxious over the recovery of her fiancé, the fragility of her emotional state compounds with each subsequent tragedy, as she's pushed closer and closer to breaking point. Can Chan wrap this mystery up before she shatters completely, or will Carol, like her brother before her, pass that point that's beyond recovery, and become lost forever in her own delirium?

But the real star of the film is the Egyptian backdrop, depicted with spellbinding awe and evocative flair via the use of stunning sets and a wonderful, colorful assortment of locals and locations; Locals such as the opportunistic Dragoman, the superstitious Edfu Ahmad, and of course His Excellency Fouad Soueida; And locations positively dripping in rich Egyptian decor. From the dark, dank, eerie quiet of Ameti's tomb, to the bright hustle and activity of the city of Luxor; from the harsh terrain of the sweltering desert, to cool, comfortable, spacious oasis property of the Arnolds. Inside or outside, day or night, Egypt is presented as enchanting yet haunting, alluring yet forbidding, brimming with life yet teeming with death. Barry and Carol, unhappy guests to the country, call it a "land of decay and death" and "dreadful place", and its superstitions, it seems, are shared by visitors and locals alike: "This household is marked for death" a terrified Edfu Ahmad warns as he flees into the night.

However, the more philosophical Charlie Chan, while irritated at times by the sand and the wind, particularly when it blows his hat away, is on the whole a far happier traveler. He even picks up one or two of the local customs along the way, with he and fellow law enforcement man Fouad Soueida perfecting their simultaneous bow/handshake as Chan hands the guilty party over to the local police. And, as he says his goodbyes, he addresses Snowshoes as "Effendi", the Egyptian term for "friend" heard throughout the movie.

When the case is closed and his work is complete, it's time for Charlie Chan to move on. When asked where he travels will take him next, Chan replies "journey of life like feather on stream - must continue on current".

BEST MOMENT: [16:17] - The discovery the victim. Professor Thurston and Tom take Chan down to their laboratory and x-ray room. Chan notices the large mummy case on the workspace in the centre of the room. He asks if it's the casket of Ameti, and is told that it is indeed that of the "powerful priest of the 21st Dynasty". But though it's Thurston and Tom, and not Chan, who are the experts in matters Ancient Egyptian, it is Chan - who we heard earlier remarking that "insignificant molehill sometimes more important than conspicuous mountain" - who notices the tiny scratches on side of the casket. "Varnish on 3,000 year old mummy case not completely dry" he observes.

Chan wants to look inside, but, assured that it's not possible for the case to have ever been opened before, is denied permission to open it now. Ever resourceful, he suggests using the x-ray machine he was introduced to moments before: "useful for seeing where eye cannot reach". Chan, Tom, Thurston and Snowshoes lift the mummy case up to the x-ray machine. They turn the lights off and the machine on, the pitch black room and the humming of the machine upsetting the anxious Snowshoes. Tom and the Professor show Chan the x-ray image of the priest inside the case.

"May display ignorance of Egyptian history by asking question?" Chan asks, wanting to know if Ameti died a natural death. Told that the priest died peacefully at the "ripe old age of 78", he replies "contradiction please. Ameti die very violent death". Holding a magnify glass up to the image's ribcage, he highlights a small detail that again only he noticed: "Modern bullet clearly revealed near heart". In light of that revelation, they decide to open the case. They remove the lid, then lift the linen-wrapped body out of the case, and cut open the wrapping to find... the mummified body of Professor Arnold!

Suddenly, the lights go out and we hear a woman scream.

IN SHORT: A riveting concoction of complex puzzles laced with neat horror touches. As much mummy movie as murder mystery.

CHARLIE CHAN IN SHANGHAI (1935)

"Instincts of detective father inherited by noble offspring"
- Charlie Chan

Warner Oland (Charlie Chan), **Keye Luke** (Number One Son Lee), **Irene Harvey** (Diana Woodland), **Charles Locher** (Philip Nash), **Russell Hicks** (James Andrews), **Halliwell Hobbes** (Colonel Watkins), **Frederik Vogeding** (Burke), **Neil Fitzgerald** (Dakin), **Max Wagner** (Taxi Driver).

Director: **James Tinling**
Screenplay: **Edward T. Lowe** and **Gerard Fairlie**
Runtime: 70 mins. 20th Century-Fox Film Corp.

Film 9 in the Charlie Chan *series.*

SYNOPSIS: Charlie Chan takes on an opium ring in the land of his "honorable ancestors".

Son (I)

Long the journey, hard the way,
But his heart was gay.
For, was he not a prince both strong and brave,
Vowed a princess fair to save?

And he slew the dreadful dragon,
Even cut off his seven heads.
And in his cave he found the princess
Bound to her lowly bed.

Then came they both back to the land
Of the mighty Emperor Fu Manchu,
To claim his reward, the dainty hand
Of lovely Ming Lo Fu.

Lively, busy, and action packed, CHARLIE CHAN IN SHANGHAI is oddly one of the more overlooked of the Chan films. Perhaps it's because it is the final and least distinctive leg of the four-part "World Tour" (LONDON / PARIS / EGYPT / SHANGHAI) formed by the quartet of successive films of which it is the last, or perhaps we simply have a tendency to take good, solid entertainment of its kind for granted. True, it's not the most completely gripping of the Chan mysteries, but it boasts loads of action and incident and plenty of smarts and heart that more than atone for any of its shortcomings.

We open with Charlie Chan on an ocean liner, entertaining a group of young children: playing leapfrog, telling jokes ("60 summers young, 60 winters old" he shivers in regard to his age), then singing to them the song of the Princess Ming Lo Fu, all in a blissful holiday mood. But this holiday mood doesn't last long. First, as he looks out admiringly at the view of Shanghai as his boat approaches the shore, someone slips a note into his pocket, warning him that "Shanghai is an unhealthy place for you. If you are wise, you will not leave this ship". Then, after arriving at the docks and conducting a brief interview with some of the local press - in which he explains that he is on vacation and in a "holiday mood" - Chan meets his hosts, who duly inform him that there's to be a formal banquet that evening in his honor. Between ominous threats and grand invitations, it's a mixed message of a welcome into Shanghai, but one can see just why Chan hasn't had opportunity to visit the home of his "honorable ancestors" in "many years". For even on what was intended to be a rare holiday, it seems that Charlie Chan cannot escape the threats of his enemies or the duties of his profession.

Nor, it seems, can he escape murder. That night at the banquet, his host and old friend Sir Stanley Woodland requests an audience with him afterwards to discuss an important matter, but before they have a chance to talk, Sir Stanley is murdered, killed by opening a booby-trapped box that was part of the banquet ceremony. Needless to say, it falls to Chan to take on the case. So much for a holiday.

Watkins: *Sir Stanley had so many friends, but few enemies.*
Charlie Chan: *Only one enemy necessary to commit murder.*

Thankfully, Chan has his Number One Son Lee, who is in Shanghai on business, on call to lend a hand, "just in case". The relationship between Charlie Chan and his son may or may not be a feature that initially attracts one to the series, but it is definitely one of the key reasons why one stays. The surprise meeting, Lee smiling and waving broadly to his father as he arrives at the port in Shanghai to greet him, and Chan's reaction, equal parts astonishment and joy, to the surprise, is so touching. And as they embrace, the genuine love and affection they have for each other - the pride old Chan has in his son, and the reverence young Lee has for his father - is as obvious as it is touching.

And whether it be in Chan's fathering of Lee, seen when paying for his rickshaw ride at the docks or when telling him "do not forget your prayers, may need them" before bed; or in Lee's relief when Chan emerges, alive and well, after the foiled assassination attempt on him; or in the "just in case" exchange later on when Chan catches out Lee following him in disguise; or in Chan asking if he can borrow Lee's detective book and Lee's broad glee at the endorsement, before realizing that his Pop is gently pulling his leg; the love and warmth they share shines through in each and every scene they have together.

Keye Luke's Lee Chan is bright, smiling, eager and earnest (with just a touch of entitlement that comes as the first son of Charlie Chan and heir apparent to the Chan detective name), playing the sidekick role with enthusiasm and aptitude, rather than stupidity and ineptitude. Sometimes he'll jump the gun, when he thinks that the evidence points to a particular suspect, and often the role is played for comedy relief, but he's always thinking, always striving, always trying to put the puzzle together, and never completely useless. If nothing else he gives Chan someone to bounce ideas off and trade thoughts with. And his devotion, tenacity and commitment are enough to suggest that he may indeed go on to become a great detective himself someday: "instincts of detective father inherited by noble offspring" proud Papa Chan beams when Lee makes an observation about the note Chan received.

In Charlie Chan and his Number One Son Lee we also have an interesting generation gap, with Chan's old-fashioned, formal manner, his stilted, mentally translated English, his wisdom, and his regard for the traditions of his "honorable ancestors" nicely contrasted by his modern, peppy, perfect-slang-speaking and fully-integrated Chinese American son. The younger, active Luke is also a great physical action proxy for the more static Warner Oland, as seen in the staircase leap he makes as Chan and Lee escape from the opium ring's hideout.

And CHARLIE CHAN IN SHANGHAI gives the Chan boys quite a workout. There's a night-time assassination attempt on Chan, that he thwarts with the old "put some pillows under the bed covers to look like a person sleeping there" trick; a thrilling abduction and escape, as Chan and Lee feel the wrath of the opium ring responsible Sir Stanley's murder; some great bits of detective work, as Chan demonstrates how an intruder can exit through a window while also locking it from the inside; a note with a message written in invisible ink; a shootout by the waterfront at the finale; and a really enjoyable denouement. There are also a number of clever little touches: We see Lee doing his morning exercises, a precursor to his physical feats later that day, and there's a brief moment with Chan and his malfunctioning flashlight that proves to be more than just luck.

When the case is over and the opium ring rounded up, Chan puts an arm around his Number One Son and acknowledges Lee's good work, to which Lee smiles and playful quotes his father's line of "Thank you, so much", and what was meant to be a holiday for Charlie Chan and son instead winds up being a very lively, very busy, but very pleasurable, 70 minutes of work.

This concludes the four film "World Tour" arc that saw Chan making the long journey back home to Honolulu after delivering a prisoner to England. Each of the four films has it's own style in keeping with the locale they depict: the authoritative and proper CHARLIE CHAN IN LONDON, the stylish and Frenchy chic CHARLIE CHAN IN PARIS, the drawn out and evocative CHARLIE CHAN IN EGYPT, and this, the busy and active CHARLIE CHAN IN SHANGHAI. Even though it's not dwelled upon a whole lot in the film, that the last stop on Chan's journey home should be to his ancestral home seems only fitting. That he gets to share it with the next generation, his Number One Son, even more so.

BEST MOMENT: [28:30] - A marvelous, exciting sequence of events. Chan and Lee are abducted and taken to the "Chief", Marnoff. Seated at a small chair at the centre of room, Chan looks up at the shadowy figure of his captor and remarks that "Charlie Chan often see enemies in shadow box. Now enemies see Charlie Chan". As Marnoff readies to commence interrogating them, Chan and Lee attempt to bluff their way free, claiming that the beggar seen loitering around outside the building is actually an undercover detective. Whether or not they completely convince their captors, their diversion plants doubt in the minds of Marnoff and the guards, who drop their guard for a split second. Seizing this opportunity, Lee punches the guard nearest to him down, then breaks a wooden chair over him as he rises, as he and his father flee the room before the other guard can turn and fire. They make their escape, with Lee making an impressive leap from midway down the stair case to knock out the last guard waiting at the entrance of the building (the image of Luke's leap was captured on posters for the film).

The moments leading up to the Chans' capture are also very well done. At his hotel room, Chan receives a note supposedly from Commissioner of Police Watkins, summoning him to see him. Sensing a trap, he telephones the hotel switchboard and asks to be put though to police headquarters so he can check the veracity of the message. "The old boy is pretty cagey. He's checking up on us" the switchboard lady, a plant for opium ring, moans, as she patches him though to Marnoff, who takes the call in the guise of the police station. It's clever writing when you can have your hero get captured in a way that still pays him the compliment of being clever. In this instance he simply underestimated his opponent's vast resources and might.

IN SHORT: Physical action, clever scenarios, and likeable performances from Oland and Luke aid this solid entry.

CHARLIE CHAN'S SECRET (1936)

"Necessity mother of invention, but sometimes step-mother of deception"
- Charlie Chan

Warner Oland (Charlie Chan), **Rosina Lawrence** (Alice Lowell), **Charles Quigley** (Dick Williams), **Henrietta Crosman** (Henrietta Lowell), **Edward Trevor** (Fred Gage), **Astrid Allwyn** (Janice Gage), **Herbert Mundin** (Baxter), **Jonathan Hale** (Warren T. Phelps), **Egon Brecher** (Ulrich), **Gloria Roy** (Carlotta), **Ivan Miller** (Morton), **Arthur Edmund Carew** (Professor Bowan).

Director: **Gordon Wiles**
Screenplay: **Robert Ellis** and **Helen Logan** & **Joseph Hoffman**
Runtime: 71 mins. 20th Century-Fox Film Corp.

Film 10 in the Charlie Chan *series.*

SYNOPSIS: Not convinced that the missing heir to a family fortune has indeed drown as suspected, Charlie Chan travels to the man's family home in San Francisco to investigate.

Truth

We enjoy the Charlie Chan films in part because we enjoy seeing a master of his craft in his element, doing what he does best, and applying his skills and expertise to outwit his challengers. There something special about seeing someone who is the best at what they do do what it is that they do best, what it is that they were clearly put on this earth to do, and of course, there's also something delightful in seeing a humble but shrewd individual confound self-important dullards who lack his imagination, and demonstrate to all with wit and clarity and irrefutable logic why his unusual theory is really unusual fact. That's one of Charlie Chan's secrets.

Another is that we like to see wrongs being righted and justice being served. Be it from Chan's initial reluctance to take on a case, or from the primrose paths that other, less accomplished, investigators seem determined to let themselves be lead down, we're often invited to wonder just how these cases may have panned out if Charlie Chan weren't around. Would an innocent man be convicted and incarcerated, his reputation ruined and his life in tatters? Would a guilty party literally get away with murder, free to enjoy their ill got gains, free from the long are of the law, free from the scales of justice? And would the truth stay buried, forever, never to come out? Even if we don't believe specifically in karma, we'd like to think that the universe will make everything turn out alright in the end, that good things will happen to good people, bad things to bad, and that eventually the truth will out. And while we know that in real life that may sadly not always be the case, having agents of truth and justice, or perhaps *angels* of truth and justice, like Charlie Chan out there certainly helps the cause.

But the real secret to the success of the Charlie Chan series is no secret. It's the character himself: Charlie Chan. This trustworthy, benevolent, and philosophical character; who drops his prepositions, but is never at a loss for words; who speaks in aphorisms, but is nonetheless always forthright; who always minds his manners, but forever speaks his mind; who is methodical and meticulous, but able to adapt and think on his feet; who picks up on everything, but accepts nothing at face value; who detects every small, minute detail, but never loses sight of the bigger picture; who is widely known, widely revered and widely respected all the world over, yet is still somehow eternally underestimated by adversaries and allies alike; who is humble and kind, but worldly and stout, and willing, it seems, to put innocent people though emotional distress if he deems it necessary to catch his man; and who promises nothing more than to do his "humble best", but whose "humble best" just happens to be very, very good.

In short, we're here for Charlie Chan himself. We're probably not here for the mysteries themselves, which, while always packed with well constructed clues and clever bits of business along that way, aren't always particularly mysterious. It's watching *him* solve the mystery that is the real appeal. Seeing him reconstructing the crime (CHARLIE CHAN IN LONDON), or determining what the evidence really means (CHARLIE CHAN IN PARIS), or explaining the intricacies of a complex mechanism (CHARLIE CHAN IN EGPYT), or tripping someone up on a bit false testimony (CHARLIE CHAN IN SHANGHAI), and getting down to the real truth. Seeing him devise a big theory that no one else considered, or zero in on a small clue that everybody missed, applying both common sense and specialist insight to the situation, combining reason and logic with wisdom and heart, and of course, dropping a few of his famous Chanisms along the way.

Sometimes the smoking gun with be brazenly sign-posted before our eyes, and other times the vital clue will be some obscure piece of information that Chan obtained off screen and didn't share with anyone least, of all us, until the denouement. Whatever the case, for the most part, we're more than content to sit back and watch the master at work, as he stuns and amazes those who accept the evidence at face value without question (CHARLIE CHAN IN LONDON), and exposes the logical holes in the theories of those quick to jump to base but hasty conclusions (CHARLIE CHAN IN PARIS); persisting with his line of enquiry and refusing to relent, even in the face of hostile opposition (CHARLIE CHAN IN EGYPT), or great personal danger (CHARLIE CHAN IN SHANGHAI).

Of course, these being whodunits, he also has to work out whodunit. Sometimes it seems as if they all could have done it. Sometimes it seems as if no one could have. But always, there is one, and it's up to Chan to sift through the coincidences and contrivances of the situation, and analyze and scrutinize the suspects - of which there always seems to be several each with their own means, opportunity and motive - to find that one. For us, a quick scan of the cast list, some simple deduction based on knowledge of the series formula, and the process of elimination, might sometimes be all we need to catch our man, while other times, it feels like we're wading though more red herrings than a communist fish market. But again, it's watching Chan do it, seeing how he does it and the way that he does it, that is the joy.

Whether it was the fate of a falsely convicted man (IN LONDON), the future happiness of a young couple (IN PARIS), or the mental health and wellbeing of a troubled woman (IN EGYPT), early films in the series concerned themselves almost as much with the drama of the characters affected by the murder, as they did with the actually murder and investigation itself (In IN LONDON, it's telling that Chan doesn't consider the case to be closed until Pamela Gray's engagement ring is back on her finger). This began to change just after the 20th Century-Fox merger, and from CHARLIE CHAN IN SHANGHAI the dramas of the individual innocents connected to the murder case gradually became, with some exceptions, more a running background item than a primary focus (for evidence of this one need only look at the difference in Thomas Beck's role between his first two Chans and his second two), but nonetheless, the Oland Chan film in particular tend to have much more at stake than just a murderer on the loose. There are people who are drowning, with Chan the only one who is able, or willing, to throw them a life preserve. And all this he does usually by simply digging for and bringing out the truth. "No time to expose lies" he says in CHARLIE CHAN IN LONDON, "Must expose truth".

CHARLIE CHAN'S SECRET is beautifully photographed by Rudolph Mate, has wonderful art direction by Duncan Cramer and Albert Hogsett, and is neatly peppered with great and on-message Chanisms (such as "Best place for skeleton is in family closet" and "fingerprints very valuable if detective can catch owner of fingers") all the way though. And who doesn't love a gothic spooky house with creaking floorboards, hidden panels and secret passageways? And all of Charlie Chan's aforementioned skills are on display: observation, deduction, creativity, ingenuity, and persistence.

All that's missing, perhaps, is that usual Chan heart. That intangible quality that elevated the Chan films above the other well-made 'B' pictures of the time, from something merely enjoyed to something loved. As it is, CHARLIE CHAN'S SECRET pleases the eye and engages the mind, but never captures the heart.

Perhaps it's because of Number One Son's absence. Perhaps it's because the person to whom we are meant to be sympathetic is a nice enough, but dotty and domineering old matriarch (wonderfully played by Henrietta Crosman) squandering her family's fortune on occult rituals that she strong-arms relatives and employees into participating in (sometimes one can't help but wonder just where exactly Chan acquires some of these "old friends" of his). Perhaps it's because everyone concerned seems pre-occupied with the wealth, while poor Allen Colby, whose possible return is of so much angst to this old money family and their hangers-on prior to the séance, is all but completely forgotten once his dead body hits the canvas, with his claim to the estate, and any potential threat his return from exile posed to their comfortable existences, dying with him. The first Chan film murder victim for whom it seems zero tears are shed, we never really get to meet him, and aside from the grudge held by Ulrich, the surly groundskeeper whose daughter was driven to suicide when Colby broke off his engagement to her, no one has much to say about his death, or about him as a person, one way or another. Even Chan, initially completely devoted to his manhunt, suddenly seems more concerned with figuring out the workings of the séance (which ultimately has little to do with the actual murder) than with tracking Colby's killer. Or perhaps it's because from this point, once Colby dies, there really isn't a whole lot at stake for anyone.

Or perhaps it's because that with all the deception employed by the murderer (rigging the phony gunman device on the church bell tower to give himself an alibi; fiddling with the grandfather clock to get Colby into position to knife him; etc), and also by the two séance operators (with all their tricks and rues in the séance room), Chan, it seems, finds himself feeling the need to resort to such things himself, lowering himself to their level, beating the culprits at their own game and out deceiving the deceivers. Here he fakes the murder of Mrs. Lowell, providing the fake sniper with a fake target, fully aware that he's putting Mrs. Lowell's two daughters through emotional anguish in the process. Then, with the aid of his "dead" confederate, they put on a phony séance of their own, employing the same techniques as the one earlier. True, Chan has set traps and used sleight-of-hand before, but always as a beacon of truth, shining his illuminating glow onto the darkness of lies and deceptions, working in light rather than in dark, with the truth rather than with lies, and tearing down other people's walls of deception, rather than putting up ones of his own.

CHARLIE CHAN'S SECRET is a bit of an oddity in the series. It fits in neither with the four part "World Investigations" films that immediately precede it, nor the four "Visiting Attractions" films that follow. Nor does it particularly feel like a bridge between the two (it's more old-fashioned than CHARLIE CHAN IN SHANGHAI, and less broad in its reach than CHARLIE CHAN AT THE CIRCUS). Though it checks most the Charlie Chan boxes, one not in the know could easily assume that it was a one-off work, rather than an installment of a formulized series (perhaps that's why it's a favorite). It does its own thing, and kind of stands alone, apart from the others.

So too does Chan, without Lee by his side, stand alone on this one. He attempts throughout to use various people as sounding boards to talk to and bounce ideas off, but without much success. From the Captain of the salvage boat at the film's beginning, who is ready to call it day despite not recovering Colby's body, to Mrs. Lowell's valet, Baxter, who won't even climb a tree without making a fuss, these potential Lee substitutes prove no substitute, while the local detectives, initially quite friendly with Chan ("we'll split a box of aspirin" they joke, after remarking on how much of a headache the case is), take an increasingly less hospitable view towards his involvement as the case progresses, tiring of his interruptions, blaming him for letting Bowan get away, then downright mocking his very presence and refusing even to listen to him at all. No one seems to be on the same wavelength as our favorite detective, and no one except for Mrs. Lowell seems to want him around, her "death" leaving him without any friends at all. Even the lovely Alice turns on him when deems him to be responsible for what she thinks was her mother's death. Alice's fiancé, reporter Dick Williams, looks early on to have the makings of a possible confidant and ally, but under the cloud of suspicion himself, he can play little part in the investigation, his main function being to serve as someone for Chan to covey the working of the rigged bell tower to when none on the police on hand are willing to accompany him.

In the end, it all falls to Chan, and it seems he has to catch his man right in the act in order to get anyone to listen to him. He restages the séance, using the same tricks and same quinine sulphate chemical as the killer previously did when they set up Colby's body, and he even allows the killer to grab the second of two decorative daggers that hang on the wall, the first having also been used by the killer the first time around on Colby. This time Chan has covered the remaining blade with graphite, and puts up a reflected image of the new target, Mrs. Lowell, (smoke and mirrors indeed), and this time the killer is caught, if not red handed then at least grey handed.

We're used to seeing Chan congenial and measured even when face-to-face with a cold-blooded killer, and even when delivering his deadly serious "You are murderer" *j'accuse* to them, but there's a brief moment here, just for a second, where, perhaps weary from how he's been treated throughout the case, from the accusations of incompetence, and the dismissive mockery from Inspector Morton, Chan really lets his captured man have it, before quickly returning to his usual, more composed self.

The murder solved and the guilty party hauled away, the resurrected Mrs. Lowell, basking in the warm embrace of her relieved daughters, insists that Chan stay on "for a comfortable visit", while the now won over Inspector Morton wants to make him President of City Hall. Chan however, pulling out his wallet photo of his wife and children, unsurprising declines, deciding instead to return home to the bosom of his family, where he is always wanted and always welcome.

Hmm. Perhaps he'll take them to the circus.

BEST MOMENT: [29:46] - After the first séance, in which the murdered body of Allen Colby suddenly appeared at the top the staircase, his face glowing white hot amid an otherwise pitch black room, and after the police arrive and examine the body and take everyone's statements, and after everyone else finally is permitted to leave, Mrs. Lowell offers to put Chan up at her home for the night, but Chan instead elects to spend the night there at the Colby house.

After a highly focused, highly engrossing, and highly full on first act, the film almost stops to take breather at this point, halting the momentum it had until now been *very* effectively generating, and going off on this little detour. With, thanks to the killer, Chan's job of tracking down Colby done, we might expect him now to zero in on smoking out the killer. But instead, Chan seems more interested in how the séance was faked than in who killed Allen Corby (the two things turn out not to be so related). It's almost a complete right turn from the main mystery, but as a scene in isolation, skeptics and debunkers will enjoy watching how Chan goes about exposing the trickery and "subduing malevolent spirits in ancient house".

Valet Baxter is "volunteered" by Mrs. Lowell to stay with Chan, as she leaves Chan to his work. But she soon returns, determined to uncover the truth. "I want to know what's going on. Where do we start? In here?" she insists. Baxter gulps and shivers and pleads for respite (Herbert Mundin serves a very important function in this film, besides that of comedy relief designate. First rule of a spooky house: For a spooky house to be a spooky house, *somebody* has to be spooked out by it, and he does the job very well), but he'll get none from Mrs. Lowell, as she leads him and Chan leading back into the séance room.

First, Chan enquires about the music that was heard playing throughout the séance. "Merely a manifestation from the world beyond" Mrs. Lowell rather grandly answers. She's less interested in the electric light fixture that catches Chan's eye - "they haven't been touch in years" she says. Chan climbs up on the table for a closer look at the fixture, notes that the very old brass fitting has a very young screw head. He unscrews it and removes the base of the fitting, to find a radio speaker planted inside. He then finds the hidden panel that houses the switch used to turn on the radio signal, a considerably less supernatural explanation for the séance music.

Watch closely Mrs. Lowell's reaction to all this: Fidgeting with her hands, gripping her ring finger tightly, then thumbing her handkerchief. Her faith, her whole world, is being shattered right before her eyes. "All our séances have been based on trickery" she finally realizes, admitting to herself the true. Her illusions shattered, her faith blown sky high, others in such a situation might find themselves broken and distraught, or possessed by feelings of abject humiliation at being conned, or even in a state of denial. But Mrs. Lowell is a tough old bird with a stout nerve, and any disappointment or bitterness is quickly doused by a steel determination to get to the truth.

With the mystery of the music explained, Chan turns his attention toward a solution for how Colby's white face shone so brightly in the darkness. Turning out the lights, he gets Baxter to stand where Corby body appeared during the séance, where the valet holds out a handkerchief Chan had previously wiped the deceased's face with. "Chemical analysis of same prove face treated with quinine sulphate solution" he explains, as a hidden lamp projects ultraviolet light onto the handkerchief, causing it to glow, as it did Colby's face.

Mrs. Lowell thinks that proving Bowan is a fraud also proves that he is a killer, but Chan insists that "finding web of spider does not prove which spider spin web". But it's enough for Mrs. Lowell - previously so enamored with Bowan and Carlotta that she went as far as to make provisions for them in her will - to voice her intention to write up a new document first thing in the morning.

But tomorrow may not be soon enough, as suddenly, in the mirror reflection, Chan sees a hand holding a gun emerging from behind the dresser opposite. He pushes Mrs. Lowell out of the way just as the gun fires, saving her life, then turns and pulls out his own pistol and returns fire.

Having survived this scrape, Chan, Mrs. Lowell and Baxter make to leave, when suddenly, they hear someone approaching. They hide behind the door, Chan with gun still in hand, as the person enters. "Oh, Fred. It's you!" Mrs. Lowell sighs with relief, seeing that it's her son-in-law, Fred Gage. Chan stares directly at Gage, his eyes boring into him accusingly. Oland's Chan may seem docile at times, but there's also a fire that burns behind those eyes, that Oland brings out only at key moments like this. "Fear for Mrs. Lowell's safety reason for visit?" he asks, to which Gage answers nervously in the affirmative.

IN SHORT: Perhaps lacks the heart of Chans, but a fan favorite, with striking cinematography and a creepy atmosphere. Put it on late one dark and stormy night, turn out the lights, and enjoy.

CHARLIE CHAN AT THE CIRCUS (1936)

"Size of package does not indicate quality within"
- Charlie Chan

Warner Oland (Charlie Chan), **Keye Luke** (Number One Son Lee),
George Brasno (Tim), **Olive Brasno** (Tiny), **Francis Ford** (John
Gaines), **Maxine Reiner** (Marie Norman), **John McGuire** (Hal Blake),
Shirley Deane (Louise Norman), **Paul Stanton** (Joe Kinney), **J.
Carrol Naish** (Tom Holt), **Boothe Howard** (Dan Farrell), **Drue
Leyton** (Nellie Farrell), **Wade Boteler** (Lieutenant Macy), **Shia Jung**
(Su Toy).

Director: **Harry Lachman**
Screenplay: **Robert Ellis** and **Helen Logan**
Runtime: 72 mins. 20th Century-Fox Film Corp.

Film 11 in the Charlie Chan *series.*

SYNOPSIS: Charlie Chan and his family are guests at a circus
whose co-owner has been receiving threatening letters. The
case turns to murder when the man is found murdered in his
trailer, with the door locked from the inside.

Family

The beautiful tracking shot at the very beginning of
CHARLIE CHAN AT THE CIRCUS - in which silhouettes of
merry-go-rounds, fire-eaters, jugglers and balloons project onto
posters for the bearded lady, the snake charmer, the strong
man, the contortionist, the trapeze artists, and the "biggest
little people on earth", midget performers Colonel Tim and
Lady Tiny, while a raconteur spruiks lyrical about all these
great attractions and more - advertises not only the wonders
that await under the circus big top, but also the stylish
spectacle that's in store for all of us.

It's from here that we really begin to see the Chan films
evolve from early talkie style of say, CHARLIE CHAN IN

44

LONDON or CHARLIE CHAN IN EGYPT, to something large, vibrant and vivid, with more pace, more punch, and more firepower than ever before. Blessed with lavish production values and strong casting, laced with style, with wit, and with care, and armed with a great lead character and a wonderful lead actor - a recipe that elevated the Charlie Chan films above the standard second features, or "B" movies, of the day - think of them more as B+ or even A- movies.

In CHARLIE CHAN AT THE CIRCUS, director Harry Lachman stylishly shows off the circus backdrop, but deftly keeps the background in the background and the investigation itself at the forefront, showing off the former, but never allowing it to overwhelm the latter. The circus color, such as Tim and Tiny showing Chan the animals, is played in short snippets, while the detecting, the investigation and the discovering, analyzing and theorizing of the forensic clues, are allow longer sequences. There seems to be more emphasis on the broad drama of the circus being in peril than on allowing us to get to know each of the suspects - whose introductions to us are swift and brief, and who perhaps get lost by the wayside until they re-emerge for the last 20 minutes - but for the most part Lachman and the writers successful juggle all the balls. CHARLIE CHAN AT THE CIRCUS is bound to be a pleaser, with all the attractions and activity of the circus on full display, and there's plenty to take in and enjoy and laugh along with merrily. This is one for the whole family.

Unusually, we have a disliked and somewhat unlikeable murder victim, co-owner Joe Kinney, who, new to the circus business, berates and browbeats the circus folk (although there is at least someone who loved him, a fiancé, suggesting he's not an out-and-out horrible person. He just believes that the only way to get anywhere in this world is with a strong fist rather than a gentle hand, with intimidation rather than persuasion. "You're wrong" the soon to be former future Mrs. Kinney says lovingly when he stops by to see her "I want people to like the

45

man I'm going to marry"). Hearing that the ape handler refuses to use the whip on the temperamental star attraction gorilla, Kinney marches over to sort that out in his usual way. His partner, the more kindly John Gaines, who was forced to sell half the circus to Kinney, and may yet lose the other half to him if he can't make good on his dues, warns him that "you can't run a circus with a bullwhip", but Kinney won't hear it. A scuffle between Kinney and the ape handler ensues, which Gaines has to step in and break up.

These scenes contrast Kinney, who is only in it for the money, versus the others - Gaines, the ape handler, etc - who "wouldn't leave the circus for all the money in the world". But Kinney's murder - found strangled in his trailer with the door locked from the inside - could have devastating consequences for the struggling circus and its crew, with local Police Lieutenant Macy determined to hold up the show - which needs to keep moving if it is to make money and survive - until Kinney's murder is solved (A direct contrast to the situation of CHARLIE CHAN'S SECRET, whose group of inheritors were all *better off* with the victim dead, and who, save for the killer and the targeted Mrs. Lowell, then had nothing to worry about).

George and Olive Branso as the circus midgets Tim and Tiny, "the biggest little people on earth", are highly appealing, nicely serving as the human face of what's a stake, and what it will mean should the circus be forced to shut down. Her sweet and honest worrying and his gruff, cigar-chomping fretting over the potential fate of the circus, and their cozy domestic day-to-day bickering in their trailer, contribute heavily to the film's overall pleasant, amiable tone.

Chan and family are in their hotel room, packing for the next leg of their vacation - a trip to the Grand Canyon - when there's a knock on the door. It's Tiny, with the news that the police indeed intend to "tie the show up" following Kinney's murder. We already know that the circus is struggling financially, and this setback may be final the nail in the coffin:

CHARLIE CHAN AT THE CIRCUS

"The circus will go to pieces and we will all lose our jobs" Tiny exclaims, anxious, not only for herself, but for her fellow circus crew, and for the surviving owner Gaines, who, unlike the murdered Kinney, has "been awful good to us", and now looks set to lose everything he's got. "Can't you do something? Please?" she asks. Her appeal reaches Chan, but he's already committed to taking his family to the Grand Canyon and it's actually his children, quite taken with the circus after their visit there, who plead their Pop to take the case: "Don't let them close down the circus" they cry. Deciding that it's a family decision, Chan says he must confer with the family, with 12 children the perfect amount for a jury, and Mama Chan as the judge casting the deciding vote. All enthusiastically cast their ballots in the affirmative, and with that, Chan exchanges his dressing gown for his suit jacket - his leisure wear for his work wear - and makes for the police station.

Just the Chan clan are, in every sense of the phrase, one big family, so too, in their own way, are the circus. There are number of sets of siblings among the troupe, as well as several pairs of married and engaged couples. They travel the country together and have been together for a number of years. Most of the crew having multiple jobs (or chores), and everyone does their part, working in unison, to keep the struggling circus moving (even the elephants are seen help push the lion cages along), while touches such as Mr. Gaines holding Tim and Tiny's hands, and Tiny giving Caesar the ape his daily banana, further give the circus the feel of one big family. The closure of the circus would of course mean the breakup and end of that family, and one wonders where many of these people would go, or where else many of these people *could* go. And so this scene with Tiny in the Chans hotel room, as the Chans elect to stay their vacation so that Charlie can take the case - his enlistment enabling the circus to continue touring while under investigation - is one of one family selflessly putting aside their own desires to help out another.

47

Though he expresses genuine humility in his own abilities, and complete confidence in those of the "distinguished lieutenant" Macy, it's moments like these where we might wonder just how much faith Charlie Chan has in his law enforcement brethren. If it's nada, then he at least has the professional courtesy to give nothing away.

And give nothing away he does. Chan isn't much of a team player in this one, keeping the knowledge that the ape hairs found at the scene of the murder were dead hairs - and his suspicions about what that and the barrel the ape used to stand on means - to himself until the final denouement, keeping his deductions a secret not only from us, but from his fellow investigators as well; our favorite detective content to watch in the wings without comment as Lee and Macy draw false conclusions from the murder scene (though he does share some of his usual great aphorisms, including "mind like parachute. Only function when open" and "one grain of luck sometimes worth more than whole rice field of wisdom"). The aforementioned ape hairs, a marriage certificate, and a signature on a photo that no one but Chan thinks important, are the big clues in this one, with Chan spending as much time locked away in his carriage with a microscope examining the clues as he does wandering around the circus asking people questions in what is more forensic and less interview focused investigation.

Doing most of the legwork is Key Luke, used once again to great effect as Number One Son Lee. The scene where he and Tim go incognito - as a mother pushing a baby in a pram(!) - in order to spy on a suspect, is an obvious crowd pleaser, but I also like the passage that follows. After his great undercover effort, he rushes back to the circus to tell his Pop what he's learned, only to discover that Chan already knows everything he has to tell him. "I'm telling you? You're telling me!" Lee exclaims, gone to great lengths and ran all over town to achieve that which Chan has managed simply by poking around the circus and sitting at a microscope. In his Chan films as a whole, and in CHARLIE CHAN AT THE CIRCUS in particular, Luke runs the full gamut from comedic to heroic to romantic. Whether its his charming pursuit of the contortionist Su Toy, who he throws over his shoulder and locks a cage in an effort to protect from the rampaging gorilla, or his eager attempts to re-stage the murder of Kinney with Macy, or his cool marksmanship under pressure as he shoots a preying cobra before it can pounce on his father, Lee may sometimes jump the gun and he may sometimes get it wrong, but he's always striving, always working, and never paralyzed by fear or indecision.

Of course, this time all twelve of Chan's kids are in tow, with the family on a sightseeing vacation of the mainland, and this provides a number of charming visual gags involving the large brood: such as the family lining up in a row from youngest to oldest to take their seats for the show, all sitting down in unison upon Pop's nod, then the baby being passed from one end of the entire row of seats the family occupy to the other.

Of course, in taking this laidback, pleasant tone, the story is lower on tension or suspense that it otherwise might be. Save for one incident with the cobra on his bed, Chan is never in any real danger, and until the operating scene climax of the final ten minutes, nor is anyone else. As mentioned, it is 50 minutes before the shrill, entangled dramas between the suspects begin to take centre stage, the film conscious that it can't cast too many aspersions on them, lest the circus troupe as a whole lose any of our sympathy, and this does make the suspects feel somewhat under developed, their stories coming a little late for the whodunit aspect to really take hold.

Tragedy strikes under the big top during trapeze artist Marie's high-rise performance, when her rope is deliberately cut, sending her plummeting to the ground, and suddenly the loud, jovial hive of activity and merriment that once filled the circus is draped with a deathly quiet. Her life hanging in the balance, we're told that Marie needs an operation immediately, but that her precarious condition renders it too dangerous to move her. So the procedure must be performed then and there, as the circus theatre becomes a makeshift operating theatre, populated not by jugglers and acrobats, but by doctors and surgical staff. Meanwhile, the whole troupe stand silently outside the operating tent, their heads bowed down in solemn wait, Chan stressing that silence is vital and that "any noise or disturbance" could mean tragedy.

While everyone waits with baited breath, Macy whispers to Chan that he's going to "pinch the whole show" if the trapeze artist dies, reiterating his earlier threat to shut down the circus. But the silence of delicate order that must be obtained if the surgery is to be a success is suddenly at risk, as we learn that the frantic, chaotic ape has again been let loose; a development that threatens to ruin everything, should the ape's blustering tornado of chaos suddenly crash into the crucial but fragile calm...

It's all very quiet yet very frantic, very delicate and oh so imperative, though it is all over an hour in coming, and may be too little too late for those who like their mysteries with more intensity, atmosphere, and thrill.

But CHARLIE CHAN AT THE CIRCUS aims to please and succeeds. It's colorful, agreeable, and likeable, with plenty to enjoy and laugh along with. It's a more all inclusive affair than the gothic CHARLIE CHAN'S SECRET, and therefore more likely than that film to be liked, but less likely perhaps to be a championed favorite; the difference between CHARLIE CHAN AT THE CIRCUS and CHARLIE CHAN'S SECRET the difference between a love that runs broad and one that runs deep.

The killer unmasked, with Chan delivering a very pristine summation, Macy gives Gaines the good news that the circus is free to go on its way, "unless Charlie here objects"; the lieutenant admitting for the first time that the fate of the circus lies really in Chan's hands, and not his. Chan says that everything is fine, though he express a desire to visit the circus at least once more, this time as just a "simple spectator". A grateful Gaines promises Chan lifetime passes to the circus for him and his family. He asks if current allotment of 14 will be enough, to which Chan, looking over and seeing Lee and Su Toy together, answers that 14 should be sufficient for now, but "maybe more, later".

BEST MOMENT: [01:44] - I love the adorable the way in which the fourteen strong Chan clan is introduced to us. As they make their way into the circus tent, the ticket collector counts each Chan with growing astonishment, as one by one, Chan by Chan, in single file from youngest to oldest, they pass him; each gesturing behind them to indicate that the one holding their tickets is yet to come: first the toddlers ("1, 2"), then the grade schoolers ("3, 4, 5, 6"), the older children ("7, 8, 9, 10"), then Number One Son Lee ("11"), Mama Chan ("12") holding the baby ("13"), and finally, Charlie Chan, with hands at maximum capacity carrying all his family's goodie bags, the full allotment of required tickets, "fourteen, including humble self", perched on the band atop his hat.

IN SHORT: Colorful, agreeable outing aims to please and succeeds, with plenty to enjoy and laugh along with. Fun for the whole family.

CHARLIE CHAN AT THE RACE TRACK (1936)

"Foolish rooster who stick head in lawnmower end up stew"
- Charlie Chan

Warner Oland (Charlie Chan), **Keye Luke** (Number One Son Lee), **Helen Wood** (Alice Fenton), **Thomas Beck** (Bruce Rogers), **Alan Diehard** (George Chester), **Gavin Muir** (Bagley), **Gloria Roy** (Catherine Chester), **Jonathan Hale** (Warren Fenton), **G.P. Huntley Jr.** (Denny Barton), **George Irving** (Major Kent), **Frank Coghlan Jr.** (Eddie Brill), **Frankie Darro** ("Tip" Collins), **John Rogers** (Mooney), **John H. Allen** ("Streamline" Jones), **Harry Jans** (Al Meers).

Director: **H. Bruce Humberstone**
Writers: **Robert Ellis**, **Helen Logan** and **Edward T. Lowe** (screenplay), **Lou Breslow** and **Saul Elkins** (story)
Runtime: 70 mins. 20th Century-Fox Film Corp.

Film 12 in the Charlie Chan *series.*

SYNOPSIS: When champion race horse is disqualified, the owner's father-in-law suspects fowl play. An old friend of Charlie Chan's, he cables the detective for help. When he dies before reaching Honolulu, Chan takes it upon himself to investigate.

Observation

From its starting gate to its finishing post, CHARLIE CHAN AT THE RACE TRACK is littered with characters sticking their "schnozola" where it doesn't belong or isn't wanted: from Lee, who barges in to Chan's office during his blood splatter lecture - ignoring the "Please Knock" sign on the door - with a hot tip of a "sure thing" at the races, to jockey "Tip" Collins, who, unsatisfied with his meager cut from throwing that same race, seeks to worm his way into a gangsters' gambling racket. From Major Kent, who, despite the words of caution of his family and friends that he's "playing with dynamite", is determined to get to the truth behind champion racehorse Avalanche's disqualification, to the gambler Denny Barton, who won't hand the threatening letter he receives over to Chan, because he wants to "do a little investigating off my own hook". "Smart fly keep out of gravy" Chan cautions Lee, but it seems no one is taking his advice this time. Even Chan goes against his own better judgment and places a bet on Avalanche.

But it's to their credit that none of them are to be deterred. Avalanche isn't actually Major Kent's horse anymore (he sold the steed to his son-in-law, George Chester) but for him it's the principle of the thing - "There's a big gambling ring backing this, and I'm going to get to the bottom of it" he insists, despite the dangers that attempting to do so may bring – and so he cables his old friend Charlie Chan for help. While for Collins, who has ruined his career as a jockey with his obvious deliberate foul, it's more a matter of necessity. He needs the money, and despite his rather small stature, he has no qualms about trying to put the squeeze on his contact, Bagley, when he later notices that Avalanche has been switched with another horse.

But as a mysterious note sent to one of the parties states: "it's dangerous to know too much about other people's business", and such tenacity and nosiness are not without their dangers. Major Kent is murdered, and we suspect a similar fate befalls Collins. Chan even cops a bullet in the leg while examining the aftermath of a fire in the ship's stables. Though it doesn't put him out of commission for long. After one night of bed rest he simply grabs a walking stick and continues on his nosy way. And it's a good thing he does, for one doubts if anyone else could have solved this one.

The film start small, in Honolulu, with Chan giving a lecture on blood splatter patterns to some fellow detectives and officers. "Murder without bloodstains like Amos without Andy - most unusual" he notes as he imparts his observational knowledge, demonstrating how, if one looks at them closely, different types of bloodstain patterns can indicate different methods of murder. We then jump to Australia for the running of the Melbourne Cup, where in an extraordinary turn of events, Tip Collins, jockey of the firm race favorite, Avalanche, blatantly throws the race - "even a blind man could see you pulled that foul" Bagley, head of the gambling ring that fixed the race, complains to jockey Collins as he pays him off afterwards. We then board the party's ship, bound for Los Angeles - which Chan joins when it stops in Honolulu following the murder of Major Kent - before arriving at the San Juanita Race Course, for Avalanche's next big race.

When we think of Charlie Chan, we're apt to fixate on his words of wisdom, but, as we see throughout this journey, he's no less effective when simply silently watching on as others speak. Chan has always been a perceptive observer of people and things; adept, not only at detecting what others either miss completely or see but dismiss as insignificant, but also at surmising what these discoveries really mean. He correctly deduces that Major Kent was killed not from an accidental kick from a horse as suspected, but from a deliberate blow to the head with a winch shoe; that discovery getting the investigation rolling and booking Chan's ticket to Los Angeles.

The night before the ship is due to reach port, there is a fire in the ship's stables. From the remains, Chan is able to determine not only that the fire was deliberately started, but also that it was controlled and not intended to damage the stables or harm any of the horses inside, the fire having been lit directly under the stable's fire alarm. He's not yet sure as to why, but he gets his answer the next day when, as the ship docks, he notices that the stableboy's pet monkey, who had earlier riled up Avalanche, again provokes a similar reaction, this time not from the volatile champion, but from another horse, lowly "palooka" Gallant Lad. "Very strange" notes Chan. "Before fire, monkey dislike Avalanche. Now, dislike Gallant

Lad" he notes to Lee, concluding that the horses travelling in the stable may have been switched, with the fire lit as a ruse to cover the switch.

He's right, though he's not the only one who has seen it. Collins has also noticed what Bagley is up to. Bagley might "fool Chester, he's half blind anyway", but not Collins, who has actually ridden Avalanche in a race, and hence knows a phony when he sees one. The late Major Kent was also right; there is a gambling ring behind all this, with Bagley at the head of it, and the ring has a new scheme for the upcoming race at San Juanita. Their plan, having switched big shot Avalanche with long shot Gallant Lad, is to place bets with bookmakers all over the country on the unfancied "Gallant Lad" at 20-1, far better odds than the disguised Avalanche would have got if riding under his own name, and clean up.

We know that absolutely nothing gets past Chan, who always keeps his eyes open and knows that "innocent grass may conceal snake", but there are a number of other observant characters sticking their nose where it doesn't belong. At the track the day before the race, owner of the real Gallant Lad, Warren Fenton, puts "Gallant Lad" (Avalanche in disguise) through a training run, to the interest of a number of people - gamblers, bookies, and competing trainers - who watch on with binoculars. Alice notes to her father that the horse doesn't seem to be running at full trot. "I told the boy to hold him back" he explains, conscious of the various onlookers, "because I don't want to advertise what we've got".

To make doubly sure nothing goes wrong with his plan, Bagley has one of the timing devices near the end of the track armed and ready to shoot a tranquilizer dart, should another horse dare to try to trump their "Gallant Lad". He also has Chan's every prying movement watched, and the detective's incoming and outgoing phone calls tapped. Then, on the morning of the race, he also has the snooping Chan and Lee abducted and brought to the gang's hideout, to be held prisoner where they can't interfere. "Stuck your snoot in the wrong racket this time, didn't you?" one of the Chans' captors remarks.

CHARLIE CHAN AT THE RACE TRACK boasts a sharp script, one of the best, and one of the more intricately put-together. There are some very nice clues for Chan to dissect, such as the watermark and type set of the real threatening letter, plus one clue that he's able to create himself, when he has Lee create several fake notes to give to various players. One or two of the film's gimmicks prove perhaps superfluous, but it's all neatly tied together at the end, and the key clue, that comes out of Chan's note passing - which will be noticed only by the very eagle-eyed, despite being thrust right before our eyes not once, not twice, but several times - is very well constructed. It's a really terrific clue, the best kind. One that you probably won't spot at the time but one think that you should have done once it's revealed.

The film is also one of the most active and incident-packed of the series, boasting two eventful horse races, a fire, an attempted assassination, an abduction, an escape, a police raid, a van of fire crackers going up in smoke, the switching and then switching back of the two horses, Chan and Lee's fun and games with the notes, and a breathless, gasping finale. We even get to see Chan punch out a guard ("so sorry, will apologize later"). And it is all aided by the punchy direction of H. Bruce Humberstone, on his first of four Chan assignments. Check out the quick swish pan crosses as he sets up all the elements for the Derby Day final act: From the stewards office, where Chester has received another letter; to Chan and Lee's hotel room, where they are abducted; to the betting ring's hideout, where the gangsters take to the phones, placing bets with agencies all across the country; to the stables, where Chester struggles to find a jockey willing to ride the cursed Avalanche; to the radio broadcasters with the latest updates on "the most exciting day this track has ever known". Occasional one shots of suspects looking guilty even if have nothing to hide slightly mar a script that otherwise plays it pretty fair, but that's just nitpicking. CHARLIE CHAN AT THE RACE TRACK is a lively flourish of a film that gallops along with elegance and flair all the way to its thrilling photo finish.

Highly satisfying.

BEST MOMENT: [28:25] - Earlier, as the boat boards to leave Hawaii for the mainland, Chan is with Fenton and Avalanche owner Chester (with Denny Barton watching nearby), when Bruce approaches with an anonymous note that has just arrived for Chester. Chester opens the mysterious letter and reads it. "Don't enter Avalanche in the San Juanita Handicap. A dead horse can't win a race" it says. In light of this latest threat, Fenton offers to buy Avalanche from Chester for $20,000, with the idea of retiring the horse to stud, but Chester, saying the note is proof that his late father-in-law Major Kent was right, is now more determined than ever to "see it through to the finish".

Chan, having watched all this, thinks he has noticed something, but wants to make sure. That evening, while Chan is having a drink with Denny and Alice, people connected with the case suddenly start to receive mysterious notes. First its Bruce, who arrives holding a note that reads "It's dangerous to know too much about other people's business". Not a moment later, the table's waiter returns with the party's drinks, and on his tray is another note, this time for Denny Barton. "A smart gambler knows a dead horse can't win" his reads. Chan asks to have the note but Denny elects to keep it himself. "I'd like to do a little investigating off my own hook"

After earlier also seeing Fenton receive a note warning him that "a dead horse isn't worth $20,000", Chan then meets Chester at bottom of the staircase when another letter is dropped. "This seems to be for me", Chester says, putting on his glasses to read it. It's a threat, telling him to withdraw Avalanche or else. Suddenly, *another* letter drops mysteriously from above, landing at their feet. This one is for Chan. Written in Chinese, the note is from Lee, telling Pop that he has delivered all the letters for him, Chan and Lee having orchestrated this round of note passing so that Chan could study everyone's reactions. We suspect that he has indeed found out what he was looking for, though we don't as yet know what that may be.

Later that evening, Chan is in his cabin bed, convalescing from his gunshot wound in the stables, when Denny enters, ostensibly to return to Chan the note he received; this action his way of saying that he deduced that it was Chan who sent out the notes (but who knows what else he may be looking for). "Whom did you expect to catch" Denny asks cheerily. "Maybe you... have answer" Chan slickly replies, not giving anything away.

IN SHORT: Director H. Bruce Humberstone's series debut. Slick, punchy, loaded with incident, well put together, and one that should keep you guessing. Highly satisfying.

CHARLIE CHAN AT THE OPERA (1936)

"Madness twin brother of genius, because each live in a world created by own ego. One sometimes mistaken for other"
- Charlie Chan

Warner Oland (Charlie Chan), **Boris Karloff** (Gravelle), **Keye Luke** (Number One Son Lee), **Charlotte Henry** (Kitty), **Thomas Beck** (Phil Childers), **Margaret Irving** (Lillie Rochelle), **Gregory Gaye** (Enrico Barelli), **Nedda Harrigan** (Anita Barelli), **Frank Conroy** (Mr. Whitely), **Guy Usher** (Inspector Regan), **William Demarest** (Sergeant Kelly), **Maurice Cass** (Mr. Arnold), **Tom McGuire** (Morris).

Director: **H. Bruce Humberstone**
Writers: **Scott Darling** and **Charles S. Belden** (screenplay), **Bess Meredyth** (story)
Runtime: 66 mins. 20th Century-Fox Film Corp.

Film 13 in the Charlie Chan *series.*

SYNOPSIS: Charlie Chan joins the manhunt for an escaped madman hiding out in an opera theatre.

Genius

A grand, thunderous, operatic symphony of music, mayhem and murder, CHARLIE CHAN AT THE OPERA is one of those old movies that epitomize why people who love old movies love old movies. It all begins, appropriately enough, on a dark and stormy night, following a title card triumphantly promising "Warner Oland vs. Boris Karloff"; a clash of titans that may not ultimately eventuate quite as we expect, but one whose mere billing is enough to instantly command our attention. An operatic overture makes way for a booming, forceful baritone, the only sound on heaven or earth that could possibly be audible over the torrent of rain and thunder and lightning it accompanies / is at war with. We arrive at the Rockland State Sanatorium, where residents "are the same as anyone else, but smart enough to admit their nuts". The newer of the two guards whose unenviable duty it is to patrol this house of the mad and the damned "likes the cuckoos", but his "jumpy" partner, who has been around a little longer, knows better: "He sings every night and it's making me screwy", he shudders, in reference to the "daffy" man inside who howls to at sky and hammers at the piano in a epic outpouring of rage and fury; a strange, amnesic man whose name nobody knows.

Inside the asylum's recreation room, a panning shot of empty chairs tells us that this man performs to an audience of none, with the sweeping gushes of the gale force wind his only spectators, and the booming clapping of the titanic thunder his only applause. Then, finally, we see him, and it's Boris Karloff. Karloff instantly draws us in with a engrossing, mesmerizing intensity. His shock of white hair, his dark, thick brows that sit atop his two large, manic eyes, and his ominous smile, bear down upon the night guard who every night brings him his evening newspaper. But tonight is not like every night. Tonight something different happens. An item in the newspaper, a notice featuring a returning Prima Donna set to star in a new opera production, triggers the amnesic man's memory and sets something off. Now he knows who he is. He is Gravelle: opera star, father, and victim of foul play. And there's something else... "Lilli!", he cries suddenly. "Lilli". Suddenly, he knows. He *must* get out. He *must* find Lilli.

But the night guard doesn't buy this sudden burst of sanity, and so Gravelle has to knock him out to make his escape. And so now, to the press, and to the public, and to the police, he is an "escaped madman" who "went violent".

And so, as Gravelle journeys to the opera house to seek the daughter he once lost, and confront those who so did him wrong, begins CHARLIE CHAN AT THE OPERA, a story of the fine line between genius and insanity, and of how the former is apt to be misunderstood and mistaken for the latter. According to Gravelle "everybody thinks I'm mad". But, of course, Charlie

Chan isn't everybody. *"Madness twin brother of genius, because each live in a world created by own ego. One sometimes mistaken for the other"* Chan astutely observes; our favorite detective one-up on all of the press, all of the public, all of the police, indeed all of us watching the film, who had mistaken Gravelle for the killer of this piece.

Back at the beginning of the film, when Gravelle was holed up in the sanatorium, the guards complained of what they took as the mad barking of the barking mad: "He sings every night and it's making me screwy". But when stripped of his straight jacket and made up into character, when removed from of the dank shadows of the asylum and put instead under the bright lights of the opera stage, what previously looked like insanity is now identified as genius, those now watching his performance remarking that they've "never heard that quality in Barelli's (sic) voice before", "it's great". Until now Gravelle has only been referred to as a "mad man", a "maniac", a "nut", but now his singing is music to the ears. Throw him in the nuthouse and he is indeed a nut, but put him on the stage, in *his* world, where he was born to be, and suddenly he's a star. "I live in a world of music" Gravelle nods in reply to Chan's theory.

Indeed Gravelle lives in a world of music, of "symphonies, operas, great audiences". And so when he attempts to relate to his long lost daughter Kitty, he does so in the only way he knows how: though music. On the piano he plays the tune he once played for her when she was a child, as he plead, begs, for her to remember. "Don't you remember this?" he cries. But of course she is too young to remember, and like the others, she too is frightened by what looks to her to be a madman. It's an excellent scene. We sympathize with Gravelle, with his desperate efforts to reconnect with his daughter and make her see the truth, but we also understand how bizarre this must all seem to Kitty, who doesn't have the context in which to put the seemingly terrifying actions of a seemingly terrifying man.

"Madness twin brother of genius, because each live in a world created by own ego. One sometimes mistaken for the other" says Chan, and perhaps they're words that apply, not only to Gravelle, but also to Chan himself. Throughout the case, Chan is paired with the skeptical Sergeant Kelly, who, like Chan, is a detective, but unlike Chan, isn't a genius ("It might to you some good to meet a *real* detective", Kelly's boss snorts), and just as Gravelle is alternatively referred to as a "nut", a "mad man", and a "maniac", so to is Chan referred to by this local detective as "Chop Suey" and "Egg Foo Yung", and asked mocking questions like "what is that? A laundry list?" Like Gravelle, Chan too is a genius of what he does, and like Gravelle, Chan's methods too are apt to appear strange to those who don't understand. When Kelly protests Chan's plan to permit Gravelle back on stage to sing as part of a plot to catch the real killer, Chan responds with a Chinese proverb, that the detective dismisses as gibberish. But later, after the trap has proved a success, Kelly asks Chan for the proverb's English translation, and then finally he understands - "I get it!". Like Gravelle, Chan too lives in his own world. But while Gravelle's world is one of music, Chan's world is one of murder.

Perhaps that's why Chan, throughout the film, is so insistent that he make his midnight boat home and return as soon as possible to his wife and family in Honolulu ("Can't be separated from that family of yours, huh?" Inspector Regan observes, more interested in discussing Chan's previous case at the Race Track and what he considers Chan's extraordinary feat in solving it). Perhaps Chan knows that he needs his wife and children as something else in his life, as something other than bloodstains and corpses, and something to keep his own genius from tipping over into madness. Perhaps that's why he sees how important it is for Gravelle too to reconnect with *his* family. In the last scene, when Chan tells Kitty that her going to comfort the injured Gravelle will "perhaps save life", he doesn't just mean from the physical wounds.

CHARLIE CHAN AT THE OPERA is apt to be held up as the standard, "*the one*"; more or less to the Chan series what, say, GOLDFINGER is to James Bond. As a murder mystery, it's arguably somewhat overrated, the middle portion in particular lacking form. But as a character piece, as a drama, and as a showcase for these two wonderful actors Warner Oland and Boris Karloff, it more than deserves its standing ovation.

BEST MOMENT: [52:39] - Chan and Gravelle finally meet. The script wisely keeps them apart until now, building up the anticipation for this key encounter, with Chan's investigation and Gravelle's vendetta only now finally converging. Chan enters the dressing room. He see the fainted Kitty lying on the sofa and approaches her. "If you touch her, I'll kill you" a voice sneers, as suddenly Gravelle appears from behind the door. Chan is cautious, but clever enough to know that Gravelle may not be as mad or as bad as he seems, and clever enough not to take what he sees at face value, even as Gravelle grabs a knife and points it toward him. "Have no intention of harming beautiful young lady" Chan answers softly. Gravelle, standing up to Chan, is suspicious. "You're lying" he says. Just then, Kitty stirs, and the sudden reminder of her presence shakes Gravelle back to reality. But the scorned opera singer feels that no one understands him, that "everyone thinks I'm mad". It's up to Chan to convince him otherwise and earn his trust.

Both Oland and Karloff are superb. Karloff's presence lend a great weight to the production all around, and while the Chan films were always well cast, it's rare for Warner Oland to have someone his caliber, someone worthy of him, to play against (see also Bela Lugosi in THE BLACK CAMEL. Lugosi and Orland's scenes together, though quite different in tone and purpose to these, are similarly an absolute treat).

IN SHORT: A rich, stylish, mesmerizing piece of drama, with Boris Karloff's presence lending extra weight.

CHARLIE CHAN AT THE OLYMPICS (1937)

"All play and no work make Charlie Chan very dull policeman"
- Charlie Chan

Warner Oland (Charlie Chan), **Keye Luke** (Number One Son Lee), **Katherine De Mille** (Yvonne Roland), **Pauline Moore** (Betty Adams), **Allan Lane** (Dick Masters), **C. Henry Gordon** (Arthur Hughes), **John Eldredge** (Cartwright), **Layne Tom, Jr.** (Charlie Chan, Jr.), **Jonathan Hale** (Hopkins), **Morgan Wallace** (Charles Zaraka), **Fredrik Vogeding** (Captain Strasser), **Andrew Tombes** (Chief Scott), **Howard Hickman** (Dr. Burton).

Director: **H. Bruce Humberstone**
Writers: **Robert Ellis** and **Helen Logan** (screenplay), **Paul Burger** (story)
Runtime: 71 mins. 20th Century-Fox Film Corp.

Film 14 in the Charlie Chan *series.*

SYNOPSIS: The sabotage of a military test flight and subsequent theft of a new remote radio guidance device leads Charlie Chan to Berlin on the eve of the 1936 Olympic Games.

Excellence

"A most illuminating spectacle: The nations of the world, about to struggle for supremacy on the field of sports" says the Honorable Charles Zaraka to the humble Charlie Chan, as the opening ceremony of the 1936 Berlin Olympic Games unfurls before them. "Yet behind all this there is another struggle going on constantly, for world supremacy in a more sinister field".

We've always been given the impression, in the films, that Charlie Chan is the very best, or at least *among* the very best, at what he does. Firstly, there's the way that other characters view him and react to meeting him. From the gasps of astonishment that the mere uttering of his name is apt to draw from those who cross his path, to the words of adulation heaped upon him by fellow law enforcement personnel whenever he sets foot in their town, it's clear that the name Charlie Chan is one that's held in high regard and great respect the whole world over.

Then there is the man himself. Not that he's one for self-promotion, always quick to dismiss these remarks of praise - saying that these others "exaggerate abilities of humble self" - but rather from the very way in which he goes about his business. From the poetic insight of his famous aphorisms, to the sharp precision of his brilliant denouements, it's clear just from watching him at work that he's a man very much in his element. It's an oft made observation that Chan is always the smartest person in the room, the best equipped person in the room, and that's absolutely true. Even when others can see a piece of evidence, only Chan is able to draw the right conclusion from it. Always cool and calm and in control of the situation, always with an ace up his sleeve or a vital clue in his back pocket when needed, Chan often seems a player in a league of his own, over and above that of both the allies, and adversaries, that surround him.

But, as he sits in Box 22 at the Olympic Opening Ceremony, it looks, for a while at least, like Charlie Chan may finally have met his match, with CHARLIE CHAN AT THE OLYMPICS pitting him against his toughest and most well resourced opponent yet.

In this Charles Zaraka we have someone who is not only not in awe of Charlie Chan, but seemingly in a different, higher, and "more sinister" field than him altogether. His words, and the tone and manner with which he delivers them, really make Chan's "humble" police work feel like a "little game" in comparison. Though he is indeed seeking to impress his superiority and mighty onto Chan, he doesn't appear to be boasting or chest thumping, but rather merely giving what he believes to be a statement of fact. Nor do we get the feeling that he is underestimating or overlooking Chan, as some people are apt to do. Rather, it seems that he has firmly sized Chan up and simply found him to be wanting.

Even before Chan meets "His Excellency", when he receives his invitation to meet him, the letter enclosed with tickets to primo seats at the Olympic Opening Ceremony, we get the impression that Zaraka will be no ordinary Chan adversary: "Gee. Box 22. that's where all the big shots will sit!" Number One Son Lee exclaims. The invitation is from a big noise also. "Zaraka. You've never met him" Lee muses, suggesting that Zaraka moves in much higher circles than our favorite detective, and while Lee is apt to be easily impressed, this time Pop seems bowled over as well.

Our first look at Zaraka, in his headquarters, sees him hovering over a chessboard, suggesting intelligence and strategy, but also power and amorality, the idea that he can control and move people as if they were mere chess pieces. When his spy Yvonne Roland arrives to deliver to him the box she thinks contains the highly sort-after "Cartwright intention", he doesn't seem all that interested in the sordid details of how the bounty was obtained, or even in the physical object itself, his eyes and attention hardly moving from the board. One gets the feeling that these grubby particulars are beneath him, that his is a higher calling, and he leaves it to his expert to verify the box's contents. Only when the expert opens the box to see, not the device, but an English-German Dictionary ("with compliments of the Olympic Committee"), only when it's revealed that a move has been made against *him*, is Zaraka's interest piqued. Roland knows who is responsible, and it's nice to hear Chan built-up and respected as an adversary, with Roland describing Chan as "the one person clever enough" to have substitute the device for the dictionary. Is Chan to be Zaraka's latest opponent - "our game is with the Oriental now" the diplomat says - or merely another defenseless and dispensable pawn, to be knocked over at will?

And now, at the Olympic Stadium, Chan meets this foreign diplomat and "big shot". And Zaraka, who has an air of pomp and frill and the grand about him, certainly looks and acts the part, taking off his hat and bowing his head ever so cordially, these pleasantries, one feels, an ingrained part of his character, but also dispersed with, beneath the everyday harmless facade, a "far more sinister" undercurrent. Perhaps the first Charlie Chan character better mannered than Chan himself, Zaraka is charming and pleasant throughout, even when his words carry that unpleasant undertone.

"This is not a game for amateurs, Mr. Chan" His Excellency assures him, confident that Chan is out of his depth on this one and should "turn the invention over to us, and return to your own little game in Honolulu". And for a while at least it looks as if he may be right. But if Chan is in over his head, he doesn't allow himself to be completely intimidated or overwhelmed, stoically iterating his intention to instead return the device to the U.S. War Department.

But Zaraka is sure of himself. That Chan, and not he, is the one currently in possession of the device, is merely an oversight that will soon be corrected, regardless of anything Chan may say or do, and he looks only a tad put out when Chan states his intentions to defy him. A chess player who thinks many moves ahead, he already has a plan ready should it be required. And it's here he proves that he isn't all just words, where, without even leaving his seat in the stadium, he orchestrates the abduction of Lee.

And now, with his son kidnapped and held for ransom, Charlie Chan finds himself deep in this "sinister field", with undercover agents, coded messages, lip reading, double crosses, hidden homing transmitters, and real and fake versions of the McGuffin to contend with, as he takes on a foreign spy ring in this excellent adventure of foreign intrigue and spy shenanigans set in Berlin, where spies of all countries of the world have converged under the cover of the 1936 Olympic

Games, in what might just prove to be his most important, most difficult, and most personal case yet.

The film begins in Honolulu, with Chan undergoing his annual physical exam and the doctor declaring him fully fit for another year of police duty. He'd better be. Elsewhere on the island, the military are conducting a test flight for a new invention, a radio guidance system for flying planes by remote control. But disaster strikes during the test, when the plane is hijacked, the pilot killed, and the device stolen.

The next several days sees newspapers and radio ablaze with bulletins of the crisis. A radio newsflash announces that "government agencies are making every effort to solve the riddle", but it's Chan and his Junior son, driving around the island for a spot of fishing, who discover the crash-landed plane on the beach (there's a nice establishing shot of the beached aircraft, then a lovely slow, tracking close up zooming in on Chan as he takes in the impressive wreckage around him). Soon the authorities, plus Cartwright, the inventor of the device, and Hopkins, the owner of the patent, arrive, and confirm that the device has been stolen from the plane. Though he draws from his local knowledge, such as when the lowest tide of the season falls, and finds some evidence, the zipper from another flying suit, to support his claim, Chan's theory that thief was not in fact the test pilot Edwards, but a second man who stowed away on board the plane, doesn't hold sway with the two experts. "I'm no detective" they say, "but it's apparent that the man we want is Edwards". Chan, who *is* a detective, is well ahead of them: "In nearby lagoon, have already located murdered body of unfortunate pilot Edwards".

The words we'll later hear Zaraka say prove to be true; this isn't a game for amateurs, and these early scenes in Honolulu suggest that Chan is very much the professional for the job. From clues as obscure as the strength of ink used on the timecard stamps at the Military base, and some strands of white fox fur found in a guesthouse (where he also finds the murdered body of hijacking), Chan manages to zero in on two possible suspects behind the robbery: "notorious filibuster" Arthur Hughes, and "lady in the white fox fur" Yvonne Roland. Learning that these suspects are bound for Berlin, presumably to try to sell the device, worth a fortune to a foreign power, under the cover of the Olympic Games, he, Cartwright, and Hopkins are duly dispatched to follow them and to find and recover the device.

These scenes show off Chan's deductive and investigative abilities, and also show him to be always one step ahead of his Chief, and able to anticipate his every order; Chan followings his Chief's directions before he's even given them, and even booking his own trip to Berlin before even being asked. Having conceded a two day head start to Roland, who is travelling to Germany on the same steamship as the US Olympic Team, and is due to reach Hamburg in just seven days, Chan's Chief wonders how he'll be able to catch up with her. Chan has an answer for that as well.

The three successive Chan films up to and including CHARLIE CHAN AT THE OLYMPICS each showcase an element of modern technology or innovation to the audience: CHARLIE CHAN AT THE RACE TRACK had the system for timing horse races: a lamp that shoots a beam of light across the track to a photo electric cell, which, once the beam is crossed by the leading horse, sends the image of the photo finish to the camera eye booth for printing; CHARLIE CHAN AT THE OPERA had the "electric eye" wirephoto device for transmitting photographic images over telephone wires, getting a portrait of Gravelle from the *Sun* in Chicago to print out on the corresponding machine rollers at the *Bulletin* in Los Angeles in just minutes; And in CHARLIE CHAN AT THE OLYMPICS we see Chan's express trip from Honolulu to Berlin, including a leg on the Zeppelin Hindenburg, that enables him to arrive before the Olympians who had a two day head start on him.

Explains Chan: "Race not always won by man who start first. Please - will leave tomorrow in company with Hopkins and Cartwright on Clipper. Honolulu - 18 hours to mainland. Then transcontinental plane from San Francisco - 13 hours across country to New York. Take Zeppelin Hindenburg from Lakehurst, New Jersey across Atlantic Ocean to Friedrichshafen - 61 hours."

Arriving in Berlin, he rendezvous with Number One Son Lee - who is there as part of the U.S. Olympic Swim Team – and together they manage to gain possession of the device, finding it inside a chocolate box stashed among one of the athlete's luggage, where it had been hidden by Zaraka's confederate, Roland. They thwart one attempt by a spy to seize the device, but later on Roland manages to make off with the chocolate box. But she doesn't get the metaphorical chocolates, Chan craftily substituting the device with a dictionary just prior to the box being stolen. And it's this clever ruse that earns our favorite detective a seat at the Olympic Stadium and an audience with the Honorable Charles Zaraka.

And it's Chan's initial refusal to hand the device over to Zaraka that results in Lee's kidnapping, as Number One Son is nabbed by two of Zaraka's men outside the stadium. In the hands of lesser film makers, the kidnapping of Lee could have been a cheap emotional ploy, but here it's played just right: very quiet, very soft, and very genuine, as the film takes an appropriately solemn turn, as if suddenly blanked in stunned, silent grief. Oland, as ever, is perfect, suitably somber and serious, and you can see and feel the pangs of his heart as he asks Cartwright's permission to use device to try and get his son back from the kidnappers, "Cannot answer as officer. Must speak as very humble father" he says, when Cartwright if he's willing to put the device back in the spy rings hands.

He tries to comfort himself in the way in which he has so often comforted others: with words of wisdom - "Ancient Chinese philosopher say 'hope is sunshine which illuminate darkest path'" - as he waits for the kidnappers to make contact, but even the ensuing ransom note with instructions telling him to be at the Stadium again the next morning is of little comfort: "11 more hours of anxious waiting". After having been given permission by Cartwright to use the device to get Lee back, he offers his gratitude, and then requests to Police Captain Strasser that he adhere to the kidnappers' instructions of no police escort, stating that this is a path he must tread alone. He slowly walks over to the door, eyes downcast, for one time in his life at a complete loss for words, and though he turns to say "goodbye" to Cartwright and Strasser he exits, it's noticeably without, as if he couldn't summon enough strength to say it, the customary "thank you, so much".

Whether it be for something as simple as the procedure for opening a letter, "envelope like skin of banana, must be removed to digest contents", or as significant as musings on armed conflict, "would be greatest blessing if all war fought with machinery instead of human beings", Chan has always had something either poetic or perceptive to say about anything and everything, and it's unprecedented to see him at a such a complete loss for words.

The three successive Chans up to and including CHARLIE CHAN AT THE OLYMPICS, all directed by Bruce Humberstone, represent the great peak of the Chan series (or perhaps the *first* peak, with the second being the Norman Foster helmed Sidney Toler films). Meticulous as the character they feature, each are fine tuned and razor sharp, but also have a sense of magnitude to match that precision. And CHARLIE CHAN AT THE OLYMPICS is the biggest of all in terms of size and scope and importance, as we go from a fishing trip and plane crash in Honolulu, to a high stakes mission on the biggest international stage - the Olympic Games in Berlin - with the film deftly blending in newsreel footage of the Hindenburg craft, and highlights of the Olympics, including the Opening Ceremony and the lighting of the Olympic cauldron, and Jesse Owens in action running in the 4 x 100m relay, along the way.

In keeping with its setting, CHARLIE CHAN AT THE OLYMPICS has a sense of occasion and a feeling of the big stage, and also a running motif of competition and excellence; experts versus enthusiasts, the experienced versus the novice, the best versus the rest.

"This is not a game for amateurs, Mr. Chan" the Honorable Charles Zaraka assures him, confident that Chan is out of his league on this one, while we're told that the lip reader watching them with binoculars from the other side of the stadium is "the best in Berlin".

Earlier, we also learn than the man piloting the plane for the device's test flight isn't the best pilot, Dick Masters, who has apparently knocked his shoulder out, but instead the second choice Edwards, who is "not so familiar with the robot". "Edwards will do alright I guess" remarks the sidelined Number 1 as he watches from the ground, the implication perhaps being that had the better pilot been onboard the plane, the ensuing hijacking may not have been successful.

With Lee already en route to Berlin, the Hawaiian portion of the film sees a new Junior son riding shotgun with Pop. But despite his audacious enthusiasm, and his insistence that he can "beat Lee at detecting right now", Chan Junior does little more than unhelpfully point out to Pop every lady in white fox fur who crosses their path. Later, the more experienced Lee proves more useful, having already intercepted the theft of an important telegram before his father even arrives. "I'm working on this case! I'm Chan and son" he later proclaims, reclaiming his title as heir apparent. Lee even has a go at a few Chanisms of his own, "as Pop would say", though he's not altogether confident in his efforts, ending most of them with "...or something like that".

And at the finale, Charlie Chan gives a denouement that's one of his strongest, as he clearly and sternly exonerates the innocent and convicts the guilty, in a summation delivered with strength and clarity and unwavering assurance. And by the end, as he sticks the landing, there can be no doubt that he is the best at what he does, having rescued Lee, rounded up the spy ring, and kept a valuable military invention from falling into sinister hands.

The film ends with Lee winning his 100m freestyle race the next day, while Pop proudly watches poolside, capping off a gold medal performance.

BEST MOMENT: [51:19] - Chan and Zaraka, with Yvonne Roland, meet in Box 22 in the Olympic stadium - a "very great pleasure" for Zaraka, a "most unexpected compliment" for Chan.

They sit down to talk shop. Zaraka speaks in oblique allusions and veiled analogies, but the meaning behind his words, as Zaraka tries to impress on Chan his strength and superiority over him, "could not be more clear if magnified by 200 inch telescope". Resting on his cane, Zaraka leans in slightly to talk to Chan. "Then wouldn't it be advisable" he suggests "to turn the invention over to us, and return to your own little game in Honolulu?"

But Chan is not going to fold that easily. "Players sometimes disregard even most expert coaching from sidelines", he counters, calmly states his intentions to defy Zaraka and instead return the device to the U.S. War department. Deeming the matter closed, Chan rises from his seat to leave, but he doesn't forget his manners, thanking Zaraka for the afternoon. And nor does Zaraka forget his, stating that "it was a great pleasure".

But unbeknown to Chan, seated directly across from them, at the other side of the stadium, two of Zaraka's men, plus an expert lip reader, watch every word with binoculars. The leader of the group scans the note page of the transcribed conversation. "All I needed to know", he says, as he goes about putting their plan into motion.

Moments later, outside the stadium, with swift and brutal efficiently, Lee is nabbed by two heavies and shoved into a black car. Betty, who witnesses this, desperately yells out for help, but none of the passersby can act quickly enough to do anything as the car makes it getaway. She rushes into the stadium to locate Chan, and finding him with Zaraka, delivers the terrible news: "Lee has been kidnapped!"

"Lee!" Chan exclaims, his eyes moving instantly toward Zaraka. Zaraka bows his head slightly and offers Chan his "deepest sympathies". Courteous as ever, he tells Chan that "If we can be of any service, please call us" and he and Yvonne make their leave.

IN SHORT: Quality caper of spies and foreign intrigue. Deftly raises the stakes at every turn. Excellent.

CHARLIE CHAN ON BROADWAY (1937)

"No poison more deadly than ink"
- Charlie Chan

Warner Oland (Charlie Chan), **Keye Luke** (Number One Son Lee), **Joan Marsh** (Joan Wendall), **J. Edward Bromberg** (Murdock), **Douglas Fowley** (Johnny Burke), **Harold Huber** (Inspector Nelson), **Donald Woods** (Speed Pattern), **Louise Henry** (Billie Bronson), **Joan Woodbury** (Marie Collins), **Leon Ames** (Buzz Moran), **Marc Lawrence** (Thomas Mitchell),**Tashia Mori** (Ling Tse), **Charles Williams** (Meeker), **Eugene Borden** (Louie).

Director: **Eugene Ford**
Writers: **Charles Belden** and **Jerry Cady** (screenplay), **Art Arthur**, **Robert Ellis** and **Helen Logan** (story)
Runtime: 68 mins. 20th Century-Fox Film Corp.

Film 15 in the Charlie Chan *series.*

SYNOPSIS: Charlie Chan investigates the death of a gangster's moll murdered for her diary of town secrets.

Wit

"Police in New York and Honolulu have one thing in common - both live on very small island. But, while we have big volcano, you have biggest 'shake-up'. Someday hope to greet honorable brothers in Hawaii, where roar of surf replace noise of subway and hot rhythm of Broadway cooled by strains of 'Aloha'".

We begin on ocean liner bound for New York City. The vessel navigates its way through choppy waters, much to the chagrin of one of its passengers, Charlie Chan, who is suffering from a bout of seasickness as a result, with son Lee's description of the lunch he missed offering him no respite. Meanwhile, in her cabin, another of the liner's passengers, a woman, suddenly finds herself trapped in her en suite bathroom, barricaded in by an intruder who rummages around her stateroom in search of something clearly very important. Realizing she's locked in, she begins frantically banging on the door and screaming for help.

Hearing her cries, Chan and Lee, ever the gentlemen knights-in-shining-armor, come rushing to her rescue. The intruder, who has just exited the cabin, feigns being a passerby, and the three of them set about freeing her. "So sorry to intrude, but etiquette ignored when lady in distress" Chan smiles as the woman steps out. She assumes she must have locked herself in accidently, but Chan and Lee point out that the chair that was jammed against the door, plus the state of the ransacked room, indicate that the incident was deliberate and that it was a burglary. The woman can't think of anyone who would do that, "who would want to rob my... state room" she says, her words trailing off when she notices the familiar face of the third man. He wants for her to check her belongs, to ensure nothing has been stolen, but she insists that she hasn't lost anything of value, "I'm quite sure of that". Chan, now in detective mode, notes that the jewelry on the dresser hasn't been touched. "Evident thief wasn't interested in diamonds" he says, though the woman claims that the jewels are fakes. She ushers her liberators away, as the other man expresses his regret that couldn't do more. Curiously, as Chan and Lee exit, she asks them not say anything to anyone about what happened, explaining that she's feeling poorly from the voyage and doesn't want to answer allot of questions. Lee, always keen to try and solve a case, is uncertain, but Chan, in the same boat as her in every sense of the phrase, agrees to say nothing.

Once alone, she rushes to her luggage to check a secret compartment in her trunk, and is relieved to find still inside a small parcel that is clearly her most prized possession and clearly the object of the intruder's desire. Meanwhile, back in their own room, Chan, still feeling a touch worse for wear, fans himself with a magazine, while Lee excitedly muses over what they just witnessed.

If it weren't for the title card at the beginning of the film, depicting bustling traffic hurtling past the bright lights of Broadway, one might think, by the look of these opening scenes aboard the ship, that a typical Chan mystery in the guise of an amicable pleasure cruise was on the offering. But, as the brassy, punchy attitude of these two fellow passengers - with lingo such as "all that excitement has my head beating like a base drum in a Harlem Band" - hint, we're heading for something a little different.

The boat docks at New York City, and as Chan and Lee and the other passengers disembark, a waiting swarm of reporters and photographers move in. "Look Pop. They're gonna snap our pictures" beams Lee, he and his Pop well used to being the guests of honor wherever they are guests. But this time the press make their beeline not for Chan and Lee, who they rush straight past, but for another of the ship's arrivals, a visiting Maharajah and racehorse owner, to whom they fling their rapid-fire questions, and it seems that Charlie Chan isn't the number one show on Broadway.

For as Chan and Lee walk down the ship's gangway, they leave behind their world of murder under the palms of paradise, and enter a different world altogether: A Warner Bros-esque gangster pic world of tough-talking hoods, sweet-talking dames, and fast-talking newspaper men; And a world populated by some of the most lively, lucid and lurid characters Charlie Chan has ever come across.

At the pier to greet them, waiting with a delegation of fellow officers and setting the tempo for this setting and this movie, is the chatty but no-nonsense Inspector Nelson. "Between murders and suicides I haven't got enough to do" he says as he marshals his troops with spitfire speed in preparation for Chan's arrival, commanding the welcoming committee with a brisk, confident ease. Nothing done by halves, there's guard of honor and a motorcade lined up for our favorite detective. Even the Police Band has been brought in, though no one's thought to check if any of them know the Chinese National Anthem, so instead they have to play "Chinatown, My Chinatown"!

Chan and Nelson meet, and such are their different worlds that they both, it seems, need an interpreter; reporter Speed Pattern translates Nelson's "Brooklyn immigrant broken English" for Chan, while Lee decrypts his father's allegorical adages for Nelson, as an invitation to a banquet in Chan's honor is offered and accepted. Speed tells Chan to call him if he needs anything, then darts off to follow another story, with Nelson left to wonder whether the ace reporter's parting words included a personal crack against him. Chan can only comment that "New York English too baffling for humble detective".

The rapid fire dialogue and lightning fast quips continue as we meet the rest of our *dramatis personae*. Two of them we already know. The woman from the liner is Billie Bronson, ex-girlfriend of racketeer and nightclub owner Johnny Burke, returning to New York after having been hushed up and packed off to Europe by Burke a year ago to avoid having to give testimony before the grand jury. And the man we saw tearing apart her stateroom earlier is Thomas Mitchell, a hood who wants to get his hands on her dairy, the pages of which contain enough dirt on the gangsters and city officials in the town to "blow the lid right off this island". After Mitchell's attempts to get it from her stateroom earlier, Billie decides to stash the diary away for safe keeping, hiding it in the luggage of her fellow passenger... Charlie Chan. But when Mitchell sees her eyeing Chan's movements at the pier, he cottons on, and as the Chans depart for their hotel, Billie's taxi follows Chan's car, and Mitchell's taxi follows Billie's: "To the Carlton Hotel", "To the Carlton Hotel", "To the Carlton Hotel".

Though she's "not looking for publicity", Billie is, within seconds of returning home, noticed by both the press (photographer Joan Wendell takes her picture despite her protests), and the police ("If it isn't little Billie" Nelson observes), and with her and her explosive diary now back in town, the other players in this show are quickly drawn in.

At the offices of the *Daily Bulletin*, oily editor Murdock pays Joan Wendell $100 hush money for her picture of Billie, then receives a call from the woman of the hour herself, offering to sell him the diary. They make arrangements to meet later that evening.

Later that evening, as Johnny Burke hobnobs around his Hottentot Club, where it's candid camera night and scores of camera hounds take snaps from every possible vantage point, Billie, furious at having been shunted off to Europe by him, arrives for a surprise showdown with her former flame. Not happy with these developments is Burke's mobster boss Moran. "She comes back when I say so" the gangster warns Burke. "I'll take care of that dame" Burke nods.

And very soon, *somebody* does take care of her. Billie is found dead, murdered, in Burke's office; the would-be canary now destined never to sing. But nowhere to be found is her proverbial song book. The diary isn't on her, nor is it on Mitchell, who is also found murdered; killed in Chan's hotel room while searching fervently for it. Two corpses. No diary.

Following every break of this thrilling double murder case is the swarm of newspaper reporters we met at the pier earlier - the murder having bumped the Maharajah off the front page - and at the front of the hungry pack is Speed Pattern of the *Daily Bulletin*. Speed Pattern, "the number one bloodhound of journalism", who has no sooner typed up and sent off his latest scoop than he's already off hunting down his next one "And wait 'til you see tomorrow's story. It'll top this one". The "freshest guy on Broadway", snappy, quick-witted and news hungry, some struggle to tell where his "brain ends and nerve begins". When Billie is murdered, needless to say, he's first on the scene, much to the annoyance of Nelson:

"You don't waste anytime getting here, do you?"
"Somebody has to protect the taxpayer. All the policemen I know are at a banquet"
"When you gotta eat you gotta eat. Have you seen the body?"
"Seen it? I found it!"
"Good. That makes you as suspect"
"Flatterer!"

All the characters tangled up in this case are strong, dominant personalities; none the type to ever back down or give an inch or let themselves be pushed around. Everyone knows their rights and no one can be intimidated. Each have an attitude and a ruthlessness that has seen them rise to the top of their respective fields, and each manage not only to keep up with the hectic pace of the big city, but to do so with a relaxed, confident ease; fully switched on, but also poised and in their element; never stopping to take a breath, but never running out of breath either. Watch Pattern's comfortable saunter as he and Nelson march to the murder scene, or Nelson reclining in his chair with his feet on the desk - at ease but also at full alert and on the job - as he argues with Burke's pipsqueak lawyer, or Joan's bouncy but taut, head-held-high certainty that her photo is "the pass key" to the temperamental Murdock's office, or the way Burke can spot a phony check instantly, or Moran's cool, confident, commanding presence as he enters the Hottentot Club.

These characters are brought to life by a positively cracking cast. Louise Henry is pitch perfect as the scorned moll Billie Bronson, returned from exile sooner or her racketeer boyfriend, or anyone else named in the pages of her explosive diary, would have liked, and determined to sing like a canary. Joan Marsh is bright and perky as the beaming, bouncing freelance photographer Joan Wendell, smiling and gliding her way through her scenes, her camera always by her side, while J. Edward Bromberg is quietly slimy and conniving as toady newspaper editor Murdock, and Donald Woods' Speed Pattern is amusingly brash and brazen with just a hint of a dark edge.

All the film is well played by everyone, save for the unmasking scene, where the killer's sudden turn after being caught out is rather unconvincing. (You also may find yourself liking the killer as a character, and being a tad sorry to see them backed into a corner, gun in hand, confessing all. Though the film has all the usual clues to the killer's identity, including and some nice foreshadowing in the dialogue and one BIG signpost, and though this is actually one of the easier ones to solve, the guilty party's identity is contrary to the usual *Charlie Chan* convention. Chan really is in a different world this time, one where it seems the *Chan* film "rules" don't always apply.)

Harold Huber, in his first of what would be four Chan roles, plays Inspector Nelson of the NYPD, combining the cynical weariness of a "been there, done that" beat cop with the broad "hands on hips" authority of a ranking Inspector, and adding a certain strength and energy that emerges from the of an excited angler whenever he thinks he's got a bite. Occasionally he veers off track, but with just a snap of his fingers he's back up to speed. Fast-talking, brash and rash, he's an interesting counterpoint for the softer, slower, more deliberate Chan. In Burke's office, while Nelson takes the spotlight, interrogating Burke and Burke's dancer squeeze Marie, huffing and puffing and putting together suppositions, propositions and accusations on the fly, we see Chan in the background, quietly poking and prodding around the murder scene, collecting details in a very different way.

"So sorry to intrude" Chan says when he finds himself instinctively asking questions and taking an interest in the case and realizes that he's stepping on someone else's mark. But thankfully Nelson is much more intelligent, and much less territorial, than some of the other detectives we see Chan come across, and contrary to Chan's earlier remark to Lee that "one room too small for two detectives", this town proves big enough for the both of them. Upon arriving at the Club to find it teeming with people taking photographs, Nelson's local knowledge that it's Candid Camera Night gives Chan the idea of having every patron's photos developed for clues. When they arrive upstairs, Nelson manages the murder scene and the suspects with authority, giving his orders and dispatching his officers to their tasks. But he's big on broad theorizing and hypothesizing - "now we're getting somewhere" he says as he seizes on every new item of testimony or discovery - while Chan, asking the coroner about the time of death and the position of the body, is more measures, more reserved, and more intent on gathering all the minute pieces before even trying to put the puzzle together. The two find common ground when Joan arrives with a photograph of the murder scene and they compare it with the rooms current state; one of them noticing that the phone, which in the photo was off the hook, has been put back on, the other that a napkin that isn't in the photo has since found its way onto the desk. Later, when Nelson finds a page from Bronson's diary in one of the suspect's possession, Chan suggests he actually read the page first, before making his arrest. "Oh, alright" he sighs.

Like the previous film, CHARLIE CHAN AT THE OLYMPICS, CHARLIE CHAN ON BROADWAY takes our favorite detective and drops him into a different genre - last time it was a spy thriller with foreign intrigue, this time it's a slangy New York gangster pic - and as was also the case with CHARLIE CHAN AT THE OLYMPICS, the action of CHARLIE CHAN ON BROADWAY is centered around an object of everyone's desire, with OLYMPICS' military invention replaced for BROADWAY with the figuratively explosive diary filled with secrets that its subjects would like to stay secret, which just goes to show that the pen is mightier than the sword, or as Chan puts it, "No poison more deadly than ink".

But while CHARLIE CHAN AT THE OLYMPICS was all about Chan, with Chan very much at the forefront of everything that was going on, driving much of the action and ultimately finding himself very personally involved in the drama, CHARLIE CHAN ON BROADWAY, with Chan less prominent, less front and centre, and rather more detached from the goings on, is much more about the other characters.

This may have been more out of necessity than choice, with Warner Oland's health beginning to become a problem. Though still a charming and eloquent presence in the key moments when it counts, Chan has one longish sequence off screen, goes other passages on screen but without comment while everyone else talks, and overall runs a little low on the usual number of aphorisms; the film depicting Chan, not as the lively, jumping jackrabbit of films past running rings around everyone, but more as a slow, demure tortoise who arrives at the finish line before all the energetic but erratic hares. Thankfully, CHARLIE CHAN ON BROADWAY has enough muscle and vigor and character about it for this approach to work, and though it's all a rather slight story, with loads of noise and activity and razzle-dazzle to distract from that fact that there really isn't very much going on, it has an attitude and a confidence about it that makes it enjoyable. If it's all a big confidence trick, then it's a pleasure being conned.

Not as lucky is Number One Son Lee, for whom New York, it seems, moves far too quickly. Eagerly anticipating the chance to get out and about in the Big Apple, he steps out of the hotel for a night on the town, only to be pick-pocketed within seconds; getting his comeuppance for two earlier scenes in where he himself was caught stealing by Chan (First, on the liner, when Chan discovers that his son had been appropriating towels from every hotel they've visited on their trip, then in their New York hotel room, when Lee attempts to abscond with his Pop's collar stud as they're getting into their formal dress).

But New York isn't done with Lee yet. Going off on his own, he manages, after some difficulty, to work his way into the Hottentot Club, only to be handcuffed and held as a suspect for

Billie Bronson's murder; his Pop having to be called away from his banquet to rescue him. He also cops two whacks to the face: First, from Burke, when the racketeer catches Lee in his office trying to reconstruct the murder, and then, from the killer, when Lee dives on him to prevent him from shooting Chan.

On the Chans' car ride to the airport after the show has closed, Lee is seen sporting a pair of dark sunglasses. When Nelson offers to show them around the city as his guests, Lee enthusiastically whips off his shades, inadvertently revealing his twin souvenirs from his visit to the big city: two black eyes. To which Chan notes:

"Evidently Broadway very hard on eyes".

BEST MOMENT: [14:50] - A fun scene at the offices of the *Daily Bulletin* between Editor-in-chief Murdock, lead reporter Speed Pattern, and freelance photographer Joan Wendell, as the three newshounds out-scoop each other over Billie Bronson's return to the city.

Speed is in the Editor's office, pitching his latest story to an unenthused Murdock, when a beaming Joan breezes in. "Hello Murdock, Hi Speed!" she smiles, as she briskly marches straight for Murdock, brandishing a large photo in her hand for which she wants $100. Murdock says she must be delirious, but Joan, knowing she has a good thing, puts her "beautiful enlargement" under Murdock's nose. Murdock gives it only the passing glance needed to affirm that it isn't worth devoting any more of his sparse time too. "I've got a dozen pictures of Charlie Chan" he says, hardly looking up. "Maybe, but if you look close you'll see a girl and it isn't Chan's daughter" Joan replies. This cryptic clue earns only a second passing glance. This time Murdock sees Bronson, but isn't any more impressed. "Billie Bronson, hey? I've got a dozen pictures of her too".

"Sure, and I've got a dozen editors who'd like to know that I took this picture today" says Joan, dropping the bombshell she knows will seal the deal. Though his demeanor hardly changes, remaining monotone as ever - as if news were merely mildly interesting rather than truly sensational - Murdock agrees to terms.

"I want you to forget you ever took this picture" he says as he takes the picture and places the order to cut Joan a check for $100. Joan can forget the picture just as easily as she can remember her way to the cashiers, and exits with her bounty. "Thanks, Murdock. So long, Speed. See you later!"

Murdock and Speed alone again, Murdock notes that Speed was at the pier and wonders why *he* didn't see Bronson. He says he *did*. "I even jumped in a cab and had a little chat with her". Now Murdock wonders why the reporter didn't tell him. Speed, always with an answer, explains that away easily: There was nothing to tell yet, but he's "going to see her tonight and get the low down" he says, referring to the appointment he has set with her for midnight.

Just then, Murdock gets a phone call. Speak of the devil. It's Billie Bronson, calling to make a deal with *him*. Murdock tells her that he'll meet her at her hotel at 11:30, then hangs up the phone and looks up at Speed with a self-satisfied smile. "I'm taking over the Bronson story" he says.

Speed, aghast at losing the scoop, pleads to his editor. "Now look here chief. I started this thing...","And I'll finish it" Murdock interjects. "And I'll make it hotter than the Chicago fire". "Okay" the put out Speed sulks. "But look out you don't get burned!"

IN SHORT: Fast paced, fast talking, if not always fast moving, entry with an attitude that never lets up. Great fun.

CHARLIE CHAN AT MONTE CARLO (1937)

"Actions speak louder than French"
- Charlie Chan

Warner Oland (Charlie Chan), **Keye Luke** (Number One Son Lee), **Virginia Field** (Evelyn Grey), **Sidney Blackmer** (Victor Karnoff), **Harold Huber** (Jules Joubert), **Kay Linaker** (Joan Karnoff), **Robert Kent** (Gordon Chase), **Edward Raquello** (Paul Savarin), **George Lynn** (Al Rogers), **Louis Mercier** (Taxi Driver), **George Davis** (Pepite), **John Bleifer** (Ludwig), **Georges Renavent** (Renault).

Director: **Eugene Forde**
Writers: **Charles Belden** and **Jerry Cady** (screenplay), **Robert Ellis** and **Helen Logan** (story)
Runtime: 71 mins. 20th Century-Fox Film Corp.

Film 16 in the Charlie Chan *series, and the final starring Warner Oland as Charlie Chan.*

SYNOPSIS: Charlie Chan and Number One Son Lee, passing through Monte Carlo on their way to Paris, are held up when a bank messenger is murdered and the bonds in his possession stolen.

Adieu

Final Warner Oland Chan film isn't one of his better ones. For starters, everyone seems irritated and irritable. Chan can't get the waffles he wants for breakfast; Lee, despite confidence in his command of French, can't talk his way anywhere except straight into a jail cell; Prefect of Police Jules Joubert can't seem to find any good help; Joan Karnoff can't convince her blackmailer, bartender Al Rogers, that she needs back the metallurgic bonds she gave him, nor get him to give her more time to come up with the money he demands; and Chan and Lee's poor cab driver just can't get his sputtering, spluttering jalopy of a car to where it needs to go, no matter how loudly he shouts at it; the contraption's calamities causing Chan and Lee to miss their connecting train for Paris. Nothing seems to be working out for anyone, and everything seems lost in translation.

Be it in the mangling of both French and English, or due to simple misunderstanding of others motives, characters inability to effectively communicate with each other leaves everyone in the film frustrated and exasperated. Lost in translation jokes are rarely amusing for the lost, and none of the characters here seem to be having a good time of it, a tone that carries over to the rest of the picture.

The mystery itself, concerning the various thefts and returns of some metallurgic bonds, isn't particularly compelling. The murdered men mean nothing to us, nor do any of the suspects, none of whom rouse our sympathies or our interest, and while the premise, a feud between two tycoons of contrasting philosophies both trying to finish the other off, and the affect their battle has on various hangers-on associated with them, might have had potential, nothing interesting really comes from it, and the case just sort of peters along, loudly enough, but without propulsion or momentum, and in a manner that is drab and unspectacular. Even Chan's usually rich well of aphorisms seems to have run dry, this one having far fewer than most (though "tongue often hang man quicker than rope" is a good one), with his best remark, "Can assist in negotiating one order of waffle without danger of arrest?" made more out of weariness than wisdom. Keye Luke and Harold Huber seem to be carrying more of the load for Oland this time too, further contributing to the film's somewhat detached and disconnected feel.

The sharp, active CHARLIE CHAN ON BROADWAY had a similar issue with Oland, but compensated for it with a chorus line of engaging supporting characters, plus snappy dialogue, some clever scenarios, and a sense that what was going on really mattered to those concerned, and wound up being one of the top Chan films. CHARLIE CHAN AT MONTE CARLO has none of these assets, and certainly nothing approaching ON BROADWAY's muscle or vigor. While one doesn't expect, or even demand, that every film match ON BROADWAY's pace and movement, CHARLIE CHAN AT MONTE CARLO never develops a tempo or rhythm of its own, and also lacks much of the joy and animation that is so evident in other Chans.

Even from the beginning, as it sets up Chan and Lee's visit in Monte Carlo and their meeting with Prefect of Police Jules Joubert, the signs aren't promising. We enter the casino, where "fortunes change hands at the flip of the card", and where, at the card table, the two competing adversaries of this piece, the "conservative" financier Victor Karnoff and the "reckless" stockbroker Paul Savarin, playing chemin-der-fer. "Money is nothing. They play only to give insult to each other", Joubert observes, but as the to gamblers stare each other down, trading veiled allusions across the card table as they up their bets ("I judge the wiles of my opponent as well as the value of my hand", etc) they each harbor a desire, and have a bold plan, to finish off the other; not only at cards, but also in business. We're then introduced to the other characters, and to see the eclectic assortment of high rollers and low rollers that are drawn to a casino, to contrast Karnoff and Savarin's big-money-but-small-stakes play with Lee's fanciful 20 franc bets and the goings-on of those more desperate for funds, such as Joan Karnoff and her blackmailer Al Rogers, might have been interesting, except that somehow it really isn't. It all seems to take quite a while to set up not very much very flatly, and a fair portion of the film has clocked by before the first dead body, of the courier tasked with delivering Karnoff's bonds, is found by Chan and Lee.

While Chan and Lee find themselves assisting in the investigation, they're never officially deputized, and never feel really involved in, or connected to, the case, merely stuck in

Monte Carlo for an extra day because they missed their connecting train for Paris so why not help out while we're here? ("So sorry, but find Monte Carlo hospitality difficult to escape" explains Chan when a stunned Joubert finds them in the police holding cell, Lee having inadvertently confessed to the murder). It all feels like a bit of a busman's holiday, and one its holidayers don't especially want to be on. This isn't one that'll stick long in the memory after you're done.

Really, there isn't a whole lot especially wrong with CHARLIE CHAN AT MONTE CARLO, there's just isn't a whole lot especially right with it either. It's unusually perfunctory, increasingly so as it "progresses". There's simply nothing special about it, no color or vibrancy or punch to it. A film set in Monte Carlo should be glamorous and sparking, but this seems to just lay there, going though its obligatory motions. The suspects are dull, the shell game they play with the metallurgic bonds tedious, and the accusations they fling at each other tiresome. "I am the police. I'll make the accusations" Joubert insists, as he tries to bring the Karnoff and Savarin's inane squabbling and demented conspiracy-theorizing to a halt, but he carries no authority, and far from controlling the situation he's just an addition to all the white noise. "For 25 years there is no murder in Monte Carlo. Then three people are killed. Like that" Joubert sighs as two more victims are found, but there's no sense of urgency or peril about it, the murders simply a big inconvenience to those whose misfortune it is to have them occur on their watch. In the end those still standing are rounded up and brought to Victor Karnoff's study for yet another round of accusations, insinuations, and insults, before Chan finally pulls the rip cord on the whole affair and puts this floundering case out of its and our misery.

There's one cleverly constructed deduction by Chan at the end about the bag with the bonds being opened with a key rather than torn apart, but it's an otherwise "let's get this over and done with" denouement in a story that ran out of wind before it even set sail. Having been found out, the killer, having gambled and lost, vows he'll be back to gamble another day, and that next time, he'll win, with his admission, as he's suddenly backed into the corner, drawing parallels to the similar scene in ON BROADWAY. But this time, before Lee can grab the killer, the killer ducks out the window and escapes, but as he flees he meets a rather unfortunate end. Meanwhile, the other suspects, most guilty of some scheme or another, are asked to cash in their chips and leave town. In Monte Carlo, only the house ever wins.

The case solved, Chan and Lee make their leave, and their ride out of town is, of course, the very same clattering, smoke-spitting stopstart taxi we were bothered with earlier. Noisy, exasperating, and going nowhere slowly, the vehicle is perhaps an apt metaphor for the film itself.

This would be Warner Oland's last turn as Charlie Chan. Early in production of what would have been his 17th Chan film, "Charlie Chan at the Ringside", Oland walked off the set, citing health issues. Granted a break by the studio, Oland returned to his native Sweden to recuperate, but wouldn't return to America alive. Contracting bronchial pneumonia, he died on August 6, 1938, at age 57.

We have 12 of his 16 performances as Charlie Chan available to us, including all of his last 11, but despite playing the character in 16 films over 6+ years, his depiction of the seemingly congenial but razor sharp detective never gets old and never seems repetitive, nor does it ever descend into caricature or self-parody.

Oland's wonderful all-round performance, and his sincere delivery of the character's many aphorisms, make his body of Chan work stand as not just a collection of mystery movies, but a philosophy, a guide to life: on how to live life, how to carry and conduct oneself, how to treat other people, how to overcome adversity and handle disappointment and setback, and how to view the world and everything and everyone in it.

It's a profound understanding, accumulated over a lifetime of experiences, a philosophy of the most thoughtful, considered, and philosophical kind, with humility, honesty, dignity, kindness, patience, and wisdom always among its key pillars.

From THE BLACK CAMEL, our only look at an early, slightly more raspy and husky Oland Chan, to the warmer, enigmatic "feather on stream" figure of the World Tour and beyond, the biggest part of what makes these early Charlie Chan films so appealing, so much more endearing and enduring that other, nonetheless well made, films of their time and type, is Charlie Chan himself. As Joubert proclaims upon meeting him at the casino, "all the world, it knows of Charlie Chan", and that's due in large to Warner Oland's enchanting depiction of inscrutable, irrefutable detective.

"Humble presence of no more importance than one drop of rain in cloudburst" our favorite detective is heard to remark at one point in CHARLIE CHAN AT MONTE CARLO. For once, Charlie Chan couldn't be more wrong.

BEST MOMENT: [44:88] - There aren't so many highlights in this one. Aside from Chan and Lee's hitchhiking - where the come across the courier's murdered body - and their temporary incarceration following Lee's inadvertent confession to the local police, this isn't an especially active Chan film, though the scene between Chan and Lee at breakfast the next morning provides some fun.

"Can assist in negotiating one order of waffles without danger of arrest?" Chan wearily asks his son as he scans the French breakfast menu. Lee, whose confidence in his command of the local tongue has been shot following the previous evening's debacle, tries instead to sway his father toward one thing he's certain he can order, strawberries and cream, but Chan is adamant he wants waffles.

The waiter arrives and Lee tries to convey to him his father's order of waffles. This effort consists mostly of him saying the word "waffle" several times, increasing louder and slower with emphasis on different syllables; an approach that shockingly enough proves unsuccessful.

"One picture still worth 10,000 words" says Chan, who has heard enough. He draws a picture of a circle with horizontal and vertical crossing lines as a representation the waffles he wants. The waiter seems to understand, "Ah, waffle" he beams, as he scuttles off with Chan's order.

A few moments later the waiter returns. "Voila" he cries triumphantly, "waffle!", as he places before Chan, not the requested order of waffles, but instead a book of crossword puzzles whose cover depicts a circular crossword image not dissimilar to picture Chan drew for him. Bon appetite!

IN SHORT: Final film for Warner Oland is slow off the blocks and never really catches fire. Not one of the better ones.

THE BLACK CAMEL (1931)
and the Early and Lost Chans

"Hollywood is a famous furnisher of mysteries"
- Charlie Chan

Warner Oland wasn't the first actor to play Charlie Chan on the big screen. Or the second. Or the third. Five years before Oland would make the role his own, George Kuwa donned the white hat for Chan's screen debut, the 1926 ten episode serial THE HOUSE WITHOUT A KEY from Pathé Exchange. Kuwa would also feature in Chan's next on-screen adventure, THE CHINESE PARROT, though this time not as Chan, with Kamiyama Sojin playing the Chinese detective in the 1927 Universal silent film, while E. L. Park assumed the part for 1929's BEHIND THAT CURTAIN, the first sound film to feature the character (and also the first film produced by Fox to feature the character), albeit for only a very brief scene toward the end of the picture.

The Charlie Chan series proper began with the casting of Oland, who would go on to play the Chinese super sleuth through 16 films. The first five of these - CHARLIE CHAN CARRIES ON (1931), THE BLACK CAMEL (1931), CHARLIE CHAN'S CHANCE (1932), CHARLIE CHAN'S GREATEST CASE (1933), and CHARLIE CHAN'S COURAGE (1934) - were adapted from the Chan novels of creator Earl Derr Biggers: *Charlie Chan Carries On* (1930), *The Black Camel* (1929), *Behind That Curtain* (1928), *The House without a Key* (1925), and *The Chinese Parrot* (1926) respectively (*The Keeper of the Keys* (1931), Biggers' sixth and final Chan novel before his death in 1933, was not filmed).

Sadly, of the first five Warner Oland Chan films, only the second, THE BLACK CAMEL, still exists for us to view today, with no known surviving prints of the other four, whose original film materials, along with those of many other pre-1935

Fox films, were lost in a vault fire in 1937. And if THE BLACK CAMEL is anything to go by, the loss of these early Chans is a big loss, because THE BLACK CAMEL is a smoldering, intoxicating, atmospheric little murder mystery...

Holes

At the Royal Hawaiian Hotel, posing as a humble Chinese merchant, Inspector Charlie Chan of the Honolulu Police summons famous fortune-teller and visitor to the islands Tarneverro to see him in the foyer.

Tarneverro arrives and straight away the meeting proves to be one between two sharp minds. Tarneverro instantly deduces that Chan is a policeman and not a "Chinese merchant" as he claims, and Chan instantly deduces how Tarneverro deduced that fact: from the pinhole left in Chan's shirt when Chan removed his police badge. They compliment each other on their abilities, though Chan has called upon the mystic to put him on notice, "supernatural powers of fortune teller make very bad smell in nostrils of Honolulu" he says, making it clear that frauds and charlatans aren't welcome on the islands. "Perhaps my physic powers may not be any more supernatural than yours" smiles the fortune-teller, who insists that in fact they are both detectives of a kind, the only difference between them being that Chan investigates the past while he investigates the future; "you look backward, I look forward" he says. Chan, as if possessing psychic powers of his own, remarks that skills such as Tarneverro's could have come in handy during the investigation of the murder of "handsome-face actor" Denny Mayo in Hollywood three years earlier; a case that still remains unsolved to this day. It's a remark to which this "lifter of veils" Tarneverro can only smile and shrug non-committal before making his leave.

But for all his talk of looking forward, Tarneverro is hung up on the past. Also hung up on the past is star actress Shelah

Fane, currently in Hawaii shooting a movie. She's fallen in love with wealthy globetrotter Alan Jaynes and wishes to marry him, but something is holding her back from doing so, and she has flown Tarneverro in for spiritual advice (as the fortune-teller readies his room for the consultation, we see that he as already obtained this recent information from an unknown source). She arrives at Tarneverro's, eager to tell him her dilemma... "Don't tell me. Let me tell you" the sly mystic interjects as he welcomes the actress, ushering her over to the two chair and crystal globe that stand in the centre of the room.

He draws the blinds, blanketing the room in near pitch black, and the two of them sit down and peer into the bright crystal globe. "I see a handsome man" he says, referring to Alan Jayne. "He asks a question" he adds, referring to Jayne's proposal. "Something stops you answering. You fear something... perhaps something in the past?"

"No! No!" Shelah shrieks in protest, for she knows instantly to what he's referring. "Three years ago" she admits, recoiling in dread. Suddenly, he pounces at her, seizing her by the arms, wrestling, grappling, trying to wring the truth out of her. He has her. He has her and he is not going to let her get away. With booming intensity, he shouts. He accuses. "I see a dead man: Denny Mayo!" he cries, commanding her to respond. Staggering slowly, as if mortally stung, she slumps back down into her chair and confesses. She was in madly in love with Denny Mayo, as was in his house on the night he was murdered...

But later, in a bizarre twist, the actress is herself found murdered, stabbed in the heart in the pavilion at her beach house. "There is old saying: 'Death is a black camel that kneels unbidden at every gate'. Tonight, black camel has knelt here" Chan says to the guest and staff of Shelah's house as he enters the investigation.

Many of the clues Chan comes across in his investigation have or involve holes: A footprint on the beach belonging to someone who was at the scene is found to have a "most unfashionable hole in one shoe". Then, when Chan reassembles the torn up photograph of Denny Mayo found in Shelah's room, he's greeted to another hole, the piece of the photo containing Denny's face having been snatched by Shelah's assistant, Julie O'Neill, who earlier also lifted the dead Shelah's ring from her finger upon her and Jimmy Bradshaw discovering her body. The next day, Chan goes to the library to trawl the newspapers archives for a completed photo of Denny Mayo, only to discover that someone has beaten him too it, with the photos that Chan was seeking having been cut out, again leaving only holes.

Aside from these, there's also the aforementioned scene at the beginning of the film where Tarneverro deduces that Chan is a policeman from the pinhole in his shirt, as well as Alan Jaynes' assertion that Chan's theory is "full of holes"

Alan Jaynes: *Your theory's full of holes - it won't hold water.*
Charlie Chan: *Sponge is full of holes; sponge hold water.*

(and, as often mentioned, there is also a hole in the plot through which one could drive an epileptic hippopotamus)

Next to Shelah's body, Chan finds the crushed remains of the actress' orchid corsage, and notes that the corsage's pin is missing. He later recovers the pin to find that part of *it* is missing, and deduces that the piece became lodged in the shoe of the killer, who trod on the corsage as they made their escape. At the dinner table, where the suspects sat the previous evening right after the murder, Chan finds scratches on the floor beneath one of the seats. Gathering everyone involved in the case back to the beach house, Chan has them sit down at the table in the same seats in which the sat the night before. Finding the person he was looking for, he makes an "odd request", asking them to remove their shoe. They do so and sure enough, Chan finds, still embedded on the bottom of the murderer's shoe, the missing piece of the pin.

He holds out the pin and shows it to the murderer, who at first exclaims "No! No!", then admits "yes", their protesting shake of the head dissolving into a quiet nod of resigned confirmation as realization sees in. The killer had learned that Shelah had killed Denny Mayo, and, after seeing the remains of the photo of Denny that Shelah tore up, simply couldn't control themselves any longer. "I didn't mean to kill her. I'm sorry" the killer, now slumped pettily in their seat, insists sadly, looking away as they speak because they can't bear to even without making eye contact, and we believe them. The denouements in the Chan films would later become dominated by Chan's long summation, but here the scene is shared equally by both Chan and the killer. That it is one of the simplest - Chan needs only to hold up the pin as testimony - helps, but it's sweetly played by the murderer and nicely directed by Hamilton McFadden.

There's a clear symmetry between this murderer's admission to Chan here, and Shelah's confession to Tarneverro back at the beginning of the film, particularly in the guilty parties respective reactions to being confronted with the truth: first rising from their chair in an act of desperate denial (both of the accusation and of the reality of their situation); a reflex action fuelled by sheer dread. Then, the rapid descent from renunciation to acceptance, where, upon soon realizing that they have been found out and there is no way out, that feeling of wound-up dread evaporates, to be replaced with a kind of wired, dismal relief, as they fall back into their seats and unburden their souls. These dual confessions align with Tarneverro's earlier assertion that he and Chan and both detectives of a kind, though of course Tarneverro was considerably more aggressive and physical in acquiring his confession than Chan is.

Nonetheless, in THE BLACK CAMEL we see a more aggressive and less compromising Warner Oland Charlie Chan, snappy and brisk speaking, with only a very occasional hint of the warmth we'd see in later films. See the scene in which he grills Judy after she's identified by the librarian, or his response after being knocked down by one of the suspects during a temporary blackout. "I am not in mood for turning other cheek, but will return assault with compound battery" he vows, wiping the blood from a cut on his cheek as he scans the suspects in an attempt to identify the assailant

Before there was Lee Chan, there was Kashimo, Chan's manic Japanese assistant, who periodically scurries in and out of the investigation; always adamant that he has found a clue when truthfully he has no clue. Like some sort of chaotic typhoon, he blusters and blunders into the room in a frenzy of misapplied energy, usually with something useless to tell Chan, dispensing his tidings before rapidly shuffling off towards his next misadventure.

Chan fans will enjoy the sight of Chan dining at home with his family - in this early outing a mere 9 children, who rattle off American slang utterly incomprehensible to their father. "I am gratefully retreating from bosom of honorable family to peace and quiet of murder case" he says to Kashimo as he exits the rowdy household for another working day.

But THE BLACK CAMEL has more to recommend to it than simply the curiosity value that comes with its status as the earliest of the surviving Chan films. For one, it benefits greatly from location work in Hawaii. "Take a moment to enjoy the palms of paradise" says local tourist bureau agent Jimmy Bradshaw, and the film really brings its island backdrop to life.

The film has no music score. Instead, the outdoor and semi-outdoor scenes are more often than not accompanied by the strains of a ukulele playing somewhere in the background. But even without an accompanying score, the movie never just lays there, thanks to atmospheric direction from Hamilton Mac

Fadden. Among the more memorable imagery: the intense, claustrophobic close-up as Tarneverro seizes on Shelah, and the shadows cast on the face of Chan as he delivers his "black camel" address upon arriving at the beach house.

But the film's primary pillars of strength are Warner Oland and Bela Lugosi, whose scenes together are a delight; Lugosi combining booming showmanship with charming subtleties as Tarneverro, and Oland making Chan a sharp, indomitable force to be reckoned with. Each time the characters bump into each other, usually in the foyer of the Royal Hawaiian Hotel, Chan is a little closer to solving the puzzle, and a little more certain that Tarneverro is somehow mixed up in it all.

While their first meeting sees Tarneverro charmingly vague about his presence in Honolulu, and their second liaison, soon after Tarneverro's session with Shelah that same afternoon, has the fortune-teller eagerly promising Chan a murder arrest before the night is out, the news Chan brings in their third encounter later that evening shifts dramatically the tone of things. Chan arrives, popping up in front of Tarneverro almost out of nowhere. Leaning in slightly, his stance silent and stoic, but his eyes a blaze, Chan stares into the fortune-teller with deafening accusation as he curtly delivers the news of Shelah's murder. Chan's demeanor has changed from earlier, from inquiring to accusing, and the mystic, who previously had the air of someone with all the answers playing coy, now seems more like someone with no answers pretending insight.

The next day, after establishing that a note to Julie telling her to remove all photographs of Denny Mayo from the library came from Tarneverro's typewriter, Chan meets the psychic again, and drops to him a BIG hint about someone not wanting Chan to see Denny Mayo's face. Tarneverro, one hand holding a cigarette, the other hand in his trouser pocket, tries to look as composed and as a casual and as comfortable as he can through all this, feigning ignorance and indifference and attempting to steer Chan in the wrong direction, while knowing that Chan suspects him of *something*, and knowing that our favorite detective has him under the microscope and studying his every word and every movement. He's not sweating exactly, but certainly feeling Chan's merciless and unrelenting presence.

Tarneverro says they are both detectives, and indeed each solves one murder: Tarneverro the murder of Denny Mayo, Chan the murder Shelah Fane. But as Shelah's killer confesses, and Tarneverro honorably admits to his involvement in it all, there still remains one killer at large: the person who murdered local artist and wrong-place-at-the-wrong-time witness Smith. As Chan moves in to arrest Shelah's killer, this third murderer, out of love for the arrested party, reveals themselves, pulling out a gun in an attempt to rescue their adored. But Tarneverro steps in, grabbing and restraining the would-be liberator, while Chan disarms them, and identifies the gun as the one that shot Smith, filling in the final hole in the mystery.

"Nobody would have known anything about it had it not been for you" Smith's killer laments to Chan. They won't be the last to do so.

THE BLACK CAMEL (1931)

Warner Oland (Charlie Chan), **Sally Eilers** (Julie O'Neill), **Bela Lugosi** (Tarneverro), **Dorothy Revier** (Shelah Fane), **Victor Varconi** (Robert Fyfe), **Murray Kinnell** (Smith), **William Post, Jr.** (Alan Jaynes), **Robert Young** (Jimmy Bradshaw), **Violet Dunn** (Anna), **J. M. Kerrigan** (Thomas MacMasters), **Mary Gordon** (Mrs. MacMasters), **Rita Rozelle** (Luana), **Otto Yamaoka** (Kashimo)

Director: **Hamilton MacFadden**
Writers: **Barry Conners** and **Philip Klein** (screenplay), **Hugh Strange** (story)
Runtime: 70 mins. Fox Films Corp.

ACT II

SIDNEY TOLER

CHARLIE CHAN IN HONOLULU (1938)

"When money talk, few are deaf"
- Charlie Chan

Sidney Toler (Charlie Chan), **Sen Yung** (Number Two Son Jimmy), **Phyllis Brooks** (Judy Hayes), **Eddie Collins** (Hogan), **John King** (Randolph), **Claire Dodd** (Mrs. Wayne), **George Zucco** (Dr. Cardigan), **Robert Barrat** (Captain Johnson), **Marc Lawrence** (Johnny McCoy), **Richard Lane** (Joe Arnold), **Layne Tom, Jr.** (Number Five Son Tommy), **Philip Ahn** (Wing Foo), **Paul Harvey** (Inspector Rawlins).

Director: **H. Bruce Humberstone**
Screenplay: **Charles Belden**
Runtime: **68 mins.** 20th Century-Fox Film Corp.

Film 17 in the Charlie Chan *series, the first starring Sidney Toler as Charlie Chan, and the first featuring Sen Yung as Number Two Son Jimmy.*

SYNOPSIS: While awaiting the birth of his first grandchild, Charlie Chan investigates a murder aboard a docked cargo freighter.

Veracity

Promotion for CHARLIE CHAN IN HONOLULU, Sidney Toler's Chan series debut, pledged the beginning of "a new era of bigger and better Chans", "more costly", with "greater production values" and "the prefect Charlie Chan".

The film cleverly opens with Chan at his home on Punchbowl Hill, having dinner with his wife and children. They accept him as Charlie Chan, and therefore we do too. Toler wisely avoids doing an impersonation of the late Warner Oland, instead making the role his own with his own interpretation of the character, and very quickly we're able to see the differences between the two.

Oland's Chan, often seen leaning forward, hands in front of him, holding his hat with his fingertips, was gentler, softer, and more inclined to offer comfort and advice, seemingly more passive though still serious and direct when appropriate. At times dour, at times giddy, but always with that profound, enigmatic "other worldly" quality to him, a quiet dignity coupled with his own personal creed, his own attitudes and philosophies towards life, love and death.

Sidney Toler, standing tall, hands behind his back, one clasped inside the other, gives us a Chan less owlish and more physically sturdy, more overtly assertive and in charge, feisty in a different way, at times cranky and sarcastic, and not shy in calling others out on their bull ("and give no further testimony?" he suggests when a suspect asks for permission to leave. If Oland's Chan was an iron fist in a velvet glove, then Toler's is an iron fist in an iron glove); a wily and experienced homicide detective, less detached, yet somehow more external to the drama and goings on that Oland's Chan was, and more ironic and less mystic. When Oland's Chan says "humble self" he really means it. When Toler's Chan says "humble self", it's a figure of speech. Both are valid interpretations of the role, and both are a joy to watch.

Toler's debut case is a straightforward plot of greed and opportunism aboard the docked freighter *Susan B. Jennings*, though one with matters at least somewhat complicated in that the ship is seemingly trawling with imposters and pretenders: We have the peculiar Dr. Cardigan feigning deafness, two men posing as a policeman and his prisoner, a woman travelling under an assumed name, and of course Number Two Son Jimmy Chan, who spends the first act of the picture impersonating his detective father. That all these people are, in one way or another, frauds, of course signifies that is Sidney Toler chap isn't one, and once he arrives, the new Charlie Chan – the real one this time - goes about one-by-one exposing these hoaxers and pretenders; first clearing up the matter over son

Jimmy, "young squirt merely chip, masquerading as block", then exposing Dr. Cardigan's deception, "when money talk, few are deaf", and so on and so forth down the line, until finally unmasking the killer.

Of course, we not only have a new Charlie Chan, but a new sidekick son as well, with the delightful Sen Yung also debuting, as Number Two Son Jimmy Chan. Though eager to prove that he can "take his (Number One Son's) place", this new Chan son, as we first see him here, is slightly shyer and less sure of himself than his elder brother Lee was. He's confident, bright and bullish when the heat is off and when the challenge is either yet to arrive or already past, but, as seen when he attempts to handle the early part of the investigation by himself, considerably more uncertain once actually out of his comfort zone and (figuratively, and in this instance, almost literary) thrown in the deep end, and Yung capably and energetically conveys all these attributes. In fitting with Sidney Toler's interpretation of the role, the Toler/Yung dynamic is different from that between Warner Oland and Key Luke. There's less warmth, less open affection evident in this new team than there was in the old. With a new, dry sarcasm on the part of the father, it's played more for humor than for heart, limiting the latter to (very) occasional key moments. But just as the two different Chans are both, in their own way, enjoyable to watch, so too are the two different father/son dynamics.

Though Toler and Yung both hit the ground running, not everything in CHARLIE CHAN IN HONOLULU is quite fully formed and not everything is quite in-synch. Toler is a little more animated and jumpy in one or two spots than his Chan would eventually be, while Yung's Jimmy would grow become a little more zealous and outspoken. There are also several halts in the story's momentum, mostly in the first twenty minutes, such as a long sequence with Eddie Collins and the lion, as well as some gags, such as the three-way telephone conversation, which don't quite work. Quirky, oddball bits of business like

Dr. Cardigan's "living brain" contraption further contribute to giving the film a somewhat awkward tempo.

In short, CHARLIE CHAN IN HONOLULU doesn't always click. But when it *does* work, when it does click, chiefly once Toler arrives onto the boat and whenever he is on screen, it really works (his interrogations of each suspect, particularly his scenes with George Zucco's Dr. Cardigan, are full of subtleties and intelligence. Also look for a scene with several successive close-ups of Chan smiling benignly as he listens to testimony that is later revealed he knew to be a lie). After having directed three of the best Oland films, director H. Bruce Humberstone returns for this his fourth and final Chan, and while this is perhaps the least distinctive of his quartet, it's as pleasing as ever, and there are enough genuine high spots to satisfy.

It would be *Mr. Moto* director Norman Foster who would come in and reshape the Sidney Toler Charlie Chans into the quicker, slicker, more streamlined affairs they would become with the next two films: the very strong CHARLIE CHAN IN RENO, and the excellent CHARLIE CHAN AT TREASURE ISLAND. But it was CHARLIE CHAN IN HONOLULU which proved that there was still life in Chinese detective yet.

Charlie Chan is dead. Long live Charlie Chan.

BEST MOMENT: [21:58] - Earlier, at the beginning of the film when the Chan family at the dinner table, Toler dispenses advice to his offspring on eating etiquette but the boisterous brood pay his words no heed. Despite what the name on the letter box outside reads, he isn't Charlie Chan yet.

Now Toler arrives on the boat, aided aboard by an accompanying policeman. Arriving just as Jimmy's cover is blown, Chan stands to one side and quietly watches the brewing ruckus, waiting to see what develops. With Jimmy exposed as *not* Charlie Chan, the boat's surly crew seize on him. They hoist him up, Jimmy crying out for his "Pop" before

CHARLIE CHAN IN HONOLULU

he even knows he's there, and it's only when they're about to throw him overboard that Chan steps in.

Where's the real Charlie Chan? Here he is. Sidney Toler as Charlie Chan in the white suit and white hat, his proper entrance to the case. That Jimmy was an imposter of course symbolizes that Toler is no imposer. He is Charlie Chan. He produces his badge and identifies himself as such.

"Charlie Chan? Then who's this young squirt?" the Captain asks, pointing to the Jimmy. "Young squirt merely chip, masquerading as block", Toler replies, his first great Chanism. Charlie Chan now on the case, Jimmy and the Captain point out to him the apparently deaf Dr. Cardigan. Ever observant and sensing a ruse, Chan pulls out a coin and tosses it in Dr. Cardigan's direction, the clank of the coin hitting the floor causing the Doctor to turn around and blow his cover. "Thank you, so much", Chan smiles, as if grateful for the Doctor's co-operation, Toler giving us his own take on Chan's signature line. He turns to Jimmy and the Captain, remarking that "when money talks, few are deaf".

As Chan retrieves his coin, young Tommy, being pursued by Hogan, comes bursting though the door and embraces his Pop for protection. *Now* Sidney Toler is Charlie Chan.

IN SHORT: Toler's debut outing isn't quite pitch perfect, but has enough high spots to satisfy, and the new Chan himself is a triumph. Charlie Chan lives on!

CHARLIE CHAN IN RENO (1938)

"When searching for needle in haystack, haystack only sensible location"
- Charlie Chan

Sidney Toler (Charlie Chan), **Sen Yung** (Number Two Son Jimmy), **Richardo Curtez** (Dr. Ainsley), **Phyllis Brooks** (Vivian Wells), **Slim Summerville** (Sheriff Fletcher), **Kane Richmond** (Curtis Whitman), **Pauline Moore** (Mary Whitman), **Eddie Collins** (Cab Driver), **Kay Linaker** (Mrs. Russell), **Louise Henry** (Jeanne Bently), **Robert Lowery** (Wally Burke), **Charles D. Brown** (Chief of Police King), **Iris Wong** (Choy Wong), **Morgan Conway** (George Bently), **Hamilton Mac Fadden** (Night Clerk).

Director: **Norman Foster**
Writers: **Frances Hyland**, **Albert Ray** and **Robert E. Kent** (screenplay), **Philip Wylie** (story)
Runtime: 70 mins. 20th Century-Fox Film Corp.

Film 18 in the Charlie Chan *series.*

SYNOPSIS: Charlie Chan travels to divorce capital Reno to help a woman accused of murdering her estranged husband's new fiancé.

Supporting Cast

"You check out of the state of matrimony and land in the state of Nevada" chimes a chatty, chipper, tobacco-spitting taxi driver to his latest fare. Like most of the cab drivers, hotel owners, judges and lawyers who call Reno home, he owes his living to divorces, and like most of those who carve out their living from the divorce trade, he can tell a first-timer from the regulars, and knows a new divorce case when one sets foot in his cab. His passenger, a timid, somewhat sorrowful looking young lady, is indeed, as hotel hostess Vivian Wells would put it, "another lost soul here for the cure", checking in for the six-week stay in Reno required to claim residency and obtain a quickie divorce. For while one may go to Monte Carlo to break the bank, or go to Broadway to see a show, Reno is where you go to sever the ties that bind.

When Charlie Chan goes on location, we want to get a feel for that location, and be shown something new, and in CHARLIE CHAN IN RENO, Reno and the Reno ethos are nicely showcased and explored. This sort of thing is needed if form no other reason than to prevent films of a formulized series like Charlie Chan from becoming too samey, and the depiction of the unique charms of "the biggest little city in the world" helps give CHARLIE CHAN IN RENO a unique life of its own. And in this instance it's better still, in that the Reno setting is also integral to the story. Whereas the localized CHARLIE CHAN IN HONOLOULU could have taken place anywhere, on any dock on any port, CHARLIE CHAN IN RENO could only have taken place in Reno.

But the strongest feature of CHARLIE CHAN IN RENO is its cast. All the Twentieth Century-Fox Chan films benefited from strong casting, with a great roster of character actors and contract players on hand to play the assortment of red herrings, jilted lovers, adventurers, local beat cops, and, of course, murderers required, and CHARLIE CHAN IN RENO has one of the series' very best:

Pauline Moore is pretty and sweet and meek and petite as the accused, Mary Whitman, found standing over the murdered but still warm body of the "other woman" set to marry her soon-to-be ex-husband. A damsel very much in distress, she's can't even bear having people looking at her like she might be a killer, let alone cope with what the consequences of being convicted as a killer would be. Exquisitely convincing, the only two things one can't believe about her are a) that anyone could ever possibly think her guilty of murder, and b) that any man would ever possibly wish to divorce her.

Louise Henry is suitably vile and malicious as the murder victim, Jeanne Bently, who, not content with having stolen the husband of another woman, takes perverse delight in what would be a socially awkward situation for anyone else. "Know her? I'm going to marry her husband" she laughs hysterically when Mary is pointed out to her at the hotel bar, before gaily strolling over to her predecessor's booth to offer her "heartfelt thanks", and to enquire about how Mary's old and her new hubby "likes his eggs". Gleeful malevolent, she raises all kinds of merry hell, and makes everyone whom she comes into contact with wish she was dead. "That woman had at least one murder coming to her", the hotel social director later observes.

Phyllis Brooks is chirpy, vibrant and vivacious as said hotel social director, Vivian Wells. "Most gratifying to meet hostess who remembers job at all times" Chan, with a mind like a steel trap, observes, when Vivian introduces Chan to Dr. Ainsley as "a detective" upon her and Chan finding the good doctor poking around in the victim's room. Clever and quick-witted herself, she instantly catches on to what Chan is insinuating, "I get it! You think I was trying to warn him for some reason" she beams, only for Chan to then make the sly assertion crystal clear: "Is there any reason to warn doctor?"

Later on, when Chan is mixing drinks at the bar for all the suspects, it's her turn to call *him* out: "that was slick, Mr. Chan" she remarks when he deftly asks Dr. Ainsley if he had ever met the victim. If not quite relishing in being a suspect, then she's certainly making the most of it, smiling and chatting brightly at the situation, amusing, alert and aware, but the only one of the otherwise suddenly glum quartet at the bar seemingly without their guard up. "Oh probably, if she had annoyed me enough" she beams when Chan asks her if she would have killed Mrs. Bently if she has the chance, as if casually tossing off a glib remark. Toler is terrific when engaging with suspects, and even better still when he has someone strong to thrust and parry with, like George Zucco in CHARLIE CHAN IN HONOLULU, and the wonderful Ms. Brooks here.

Kay Linaker, who is as effective as always as Mrs. Russell, the compassionate but no-nonsense hotel landlady with the unenviable task of keeping the peace in this house where it seems anything can happen, and **Iris Wong,** who is lovely as the victim's young maid, Choy Wong, round out the female players. Both are good here and would be even better still in their larger roles in the later film CHARLIE CHAN IN RIO.

Though it's the women who shine brightest in this one ("Man yet to be born who can tell what woman will or will not do" says Chan), their male counterparts are not to be completely outdone. **Richardo Curtez** provides a tall, dark and smooth sheen to the slippery and superficially charming Dr. Ainsley, giving this stock character life and making him stand out much more than he otherwise might have. A recurring problem with other mystery titles is their failure to adequately distinguish their various suspects from each other, and when the viewer can't differentiate who's who, there's naturally little interest in who did it. This is never an issue when you have actors like Richardo Curtez around.

Kane Richmond makes for a stanch and comforting matinee idol shoulder to lean on as Curtis Whitman, husband of the accused and fiancé of the victim. "Is concern for living or for dead?" Chan asks when Curtis comes to Chan's office pleading for his help. "Mary is still my wife, despite what we had planned" he asserts, his genuine concern for his still present wife and his sense of responsibility (and love) toward her shining though. Meanwhile, **Robert Lowery** adds another interesting suspect to the mix with his acute turn as the victim's jilted ex, the somewhat pitiful and dismal Wally Burke.

Slim Summerville has fun with the role Tombstone Fletcher, the local detective who never gets his man; who jumps to rash judgments and insists he has the case in hand, but is somehow always one step behind; who is so zealous that he tries to arrest someone already under arrest, yet so laconic that he doesn't even recognize the name of his number one suspect when he hears it. The device of pairing Chan up with a local detective, either one who holds him in adulation (e.g. CHARLIE CHAN AT MONTE CARLO) or one skeptical of his methods (e.g. CHARLIE CHAN AT THE OPERA) (but in either case generally a bit thick), was semi-regular staple of the Warner Oland Chan films, but would become a less frequently employed tool in the Tolers (perhaps because Toler comes across as more immediately intimidating and less likely to be underestimated). But here the teaming is a success, with Fletcher and Chan trading wry barbs and sly digs, and though "Tombstone" definitely takes his lumps, he gets a few good jabs in himself.

Eddie Collins as the chatty taxi-driver mentioned earlier, who, like many of his fellow Reno inhabitants, makes his living off the divorce trade, deftly helps set the scene. All in all the humor is far better blended into the story and setting here than was the case in the stopstart CHARLIE CHAN IN HONOLULU.

Sen Yung's Number Two Son is still a tad shyer and tentative - seen here attempting to accelerate his own maturity by way of smoking - but he's still also ever the eager-beaver, with a bounding confidence and belief that with him helping out, the case will be "cleared up in no time". Imposing himself on to the investigation, Jimmy is probably a bit too counterproductive here, hiding one piece of evidence - a burn mark on the carpet he thinks that he caused - and, out of misplaced initiative, manufacturing another, planting scissors similar to the murder weapon in everybody's room. But an after an inauspicious start (that begins with him getting robbed of his car and his clothes, then pulled out of a police line-up by none other than his astonished Pop), he comes good at the end with his knowledge of chemistry and nitric acid proving crucial to solving the case.

The great supporting players, many of who would appear again in later Chans, raise CHARLIE CHAN IN RENO from above average to *above* above average, but one would be remiss not to also make mention of the film's star, **Sidney Toler**, who, with a strength and presence that dominates every scene he's in, solidifies himself as the new Charlie Chan. Whether it's interviewing suspects, comforting witnesses, discovering clues, tut-tutting over his Number Two son, bickering with the Sherriff, or simply pleading for patience, Toler again proves himself a great and, in his own way, charming, Charlie Chan. A particular highlight is the scene in which he plays bartender for the suspects, his intelligence and wry guile really shining through. "Praise in any language very sweet".

With good actors, plus smart dialogue, a fun, albeit slight, premise, and slick direction from Norman Foster, CHARLIE CHAN IN RENO is an overall smoother, stronger, cleverer, better paced, more consistent and more self-assured film than CHARLIE CHAN IN HONOLULU. There's also a trip to a ghost town in the dead of night, in which Chan and Fletcher tackle an elusive suspect and each other.

It's a highly pleasing journey, right up until its slightly underwhelming destination, with the final unmasking - in which the suspects are required to don the same clothing they wore on the night of murder - presented without passion, suspense or thrill, or a really potent motive on behalf of the guilty party (though at least this time the scandalous past history of the suspects and their prior interrelationships are revealed to us *before* the denouement scene). But overall CHARLIE CHAN IN RENO is a strong marriage of all that we love about Charlie Chan. This one's a keeper.

BEST MOMENT: [30:52] - Chan plays bartender, throwing a party for suspects Wally Burke, Vivian Wells, Dr. Ainsley, and Mrs. Russell. All the actors are in fine form, particularly Toler and Phyllis Brooks. "What's in it, Mr. Chan? Something to loosen the tongue?" Ms. Wells asks as he pours her the drink he made. One-by-one, Chan slyly draws out everyone's feeling about the victim and whether they had ever met her previously. Ms. Wells, alert to what he's doing and ever upfront, asks "If you're trying to find someone who knew her before she came here, why don't you just ask?", "Have already asked" Chan smiles charmingly (I love too that Chan seems to be enjoying himself. Why shouldn't Chan enjoy his work?).

Just then Mary and Curtis enter the room, sitting down at a booth, presumably as Chan had planned. Seeing them come in, reality hits, and suddenly the others are not reveling in the situation as much as Vivian and Chan. Soon everyone is accusing each other and feeling accused themselves, culminating in a punch-up between Burke and Dr. Ainsley. "You knew he was throwing a party but did you know he was staging a riot?" a bewildered Tombstone asks his chief over the phone before intervening in the melee, only to get himself punched out for all his trouble.

IN SHORT: Well cast mystery with its own unique lingo and sense of place. Strong acting and direction overcome story weaknesses. Above average.

CHARLIE CHAN
AT TREASURE ISLAND (1939)

"Sometimes black magic very close relative to blackmail"
- Charlie Chan

Sidney Toler (Charlie Chan), **Sen Yung** (Number Two Son Jimmy), **Cesar Romero** (Rhadini), **Pauline Moore** (Eve Cairo), **Douglas Fowley** (Pete Lewis), **June Gale** (Myra Rhadini), **Douglas Dumbrille** (Thomas Gregory), **Sally Blane** (Stella Essex), **Billie Seward** (Bessie Sibley), **Wally Vernon** (Elmer Kelner), **Donald MacBride** (Chief J.J. Kilvaine), **Charles Halton** (Redley), **Trevor Bardette** (Abdul), **Louis Jean Heydt** (Paul Essex).

Director: **Norman Foster**
Screenplay: **John Larkin**
Runtime: 75 mins. 20th Century-Fox Film Corp.

Film 19 in the Charlie Chan *series.*

SYNOPSIS: Charlie Chan suspects a mysterious psychic of being responsible for the suicide of a friend.

Grandeur

Older, wiser, better Charlie Chan devotees than I, long ago proclaimed CHARLIE CHAN AT TREASURE ISLAND to be one of the best, if not the best, of the series. And having come to this same conclusion as those who arrived much earlier, what can this late comer to the party and last on the bandwagon possibly add, but to cry out a hearty "hear, hear", and cast yet another vote in the affirmative to be added to the already overflowing box of ballots in its favor? Because CHARLIE CHAN AT TREASURE ISLAND is undeniably the grandest of the Chan films. Everything about it, from Chan's China Clipper ride into stormy weather in the film's opening, to Chan and his companions' first attempt at infiltrating the mysterious Dr. Zodiac's lair, to the daring finale onstage at the Temple of Magic, somehow feels bigger, better, more important than anything in a Chan film before or since. There's a splendor and magnificence, but also a strength and sense of enormity, to it all. And it never lets up, the film culminating in an enthralling climax that fittingly takes place on a big theatre stage in front of a packed house.

Every scene in the film is delivered with punch, potency and vigor, and though I'll endeavor to give it the full rundown it deserves, I'd like to focus mainly on a quartet of key passages I feel particularly exemplify why CHARLIE CHAN AT TREASURE ISLAND stands over and above most of the other Chans. The four scenes are: 1) Chan breaking the news of Paul Essex's death to Essex's widow; 2) Chan and co.'s discovery of the blackmailing racket and Chan's decision to destroy key evidence; 3) Chan's psychological analysis of Dr. Zodiac; and 4) the finale at the Temple of Magic.

The film begins with Charlie Chan and Number Two Son Jimmy on the China Clipper on their way to San Francisco. Also aboard the plane is Chan's friend, mystery writer Paul Essex, who has just finished work on his latest book, "The Secret of the Pigmy Arrow", a novel about a phony mystic. Just as he slips the completed manuscript into his briefcase, the writer receives a mysterious radiogram, the contents of which seem to distress him.

He asks Chan what day the sign of Scorpio begins. Chan tells him that tomorrow is the first day of Scorpio. Surprised by the question, Chan asks Essex if he believes in astrology. "No" Essex answers, his focus still on the radiogram, "this is something else". Chan senses that something is wrong and offers his help, but Essex is evasive on the subject.

Later, as the plane is landing, Essex is found dead, having committed suicide. Chan reads the radiogram he suspects drove Essex to ending his life: "SIGN OF SCORPIO INDICATES DISASTER IF ZODIAC OBLIGATIONS NOT MET". The plane lands and what follows is a very nice character moment, genuine and heartfelt, of Chan having to deliver the news of Paul Essex's death to his waiting widow at the airport. "Paul's wife. If she's there to meet him, what are you going to tell her?" Jimmy asks his father as they exit the plane. "Only that which comes from heart" Chan answers, said heart already very heavy with the news he has to deliver.

We see Mrs. Essex waiting, with her uncle and the loved ones of other arrivals, at the airport gate. She spots Chan and cheerfully waves him over, expecting her husband to be not far behind him. When Chan reaches the gate, he's finds her agog with excitement and anticipation for her impending reunion with her spouse, who it's clear that she's missed during his absence this last month. "Impossible to miss someone who will always be in heart" Chan offers, but she's only half paying attention, her eyes still scanning around the terminal for her husband. "Where's Paul?" she begins to wonder as the last of plane's passengers has walked past. "Wish tongue could find words" starts Chan, as he tries his best to answer, but is unable to get the simple words out, and can instead only hide behind his parables. As the covered corpse of Paul Essex is carried away on a stretcher, and Mrs. Essex and her uncle puts the pieces together, it falls to the uncle to say the words "he's dead". Chan nods and looks down solemnly.

It's tasteful and understated and real and true and very well done. A real person has been killed and he has left real people behind, a devoted and loving young wife no less. The scene is cleverly staged, with Chan and Mrs. Essex separated and divided by the airport fence as he tries to give her the news. Of course, this is a Chan film, and every Chan film has at least one murder, but somehow in CHARLIE CHAN AT TREASURE ISLAND these same events seem bigger and more important than they ever have been before.

Not only the events, but the people as well. From the moment he magically appears in Police Chief Kilvaine's office,

Cesar Romero as Rhadini, the illusionist and psychic debunker who has set his sights on exposing Zodiac, proves to be one of the more charismatic and dominant Chan guest stars ever. Bringing the showmanship, excitement and enthusiasm of the character to life, he's charming and clever with a hint of something else, and with very simple facial expressions that somehow suggest that lot going on in the mind behind them.

Rhadini and newspaper reporter Pete Lewis have together been on a crusade exposing fraudulent spiritualist and charlatans of the occult. After several big successes, they're now set their sights on their biggest target yet, the famous Dr. Zodiac, but so far they've been able to lure the elusive mystic out into the open. Watch how they barrage Chan with an excited frenzy of questions when he mentions the death of Essex, thinking that Chan may have a found a connection between Essex and Zodiac, and you can see how important it is to them. They're keen bordering on fanatic.

Chan learns from Rhadini and Lewis that three other people, all clients of Dr. Zodiac, have also recently committed suicide. Suddenly Essex's radiogram and suicide make sense, "Zodiac" referring not to astrology, but to the mystic, and the "obligation" a payoff. "Sometimes black magic very close relative to blackmail" Chan explains. In Chan's opinion, "suicide induced by blackmail is murder".

But for all the film's scope and magnitude, there are loads of nice little touches as well. When Chan, Rhadini and Lewis make their first visit to Dr. Zodiac's mansion, during the day, we see Zodiac's assistant, the "Turk", peering through the curtain of an upper story window as they arrive, along with a black cat perched on the window sill.

As the Turk ushers the visitors in, leading them into a room that's draped in black, Chan and Rhadini notice some of the props and pieces, including a Persian sacrificial knife, all authentic, that lay within. Suddenly, a gong is heard and the big, broad, bellowing, bearded figure of Dr. Zodiac emerges (complete with a turban on his head, and, my favorite touch, the signs of the zodiac on his ceremonial frill). Zodiac and his guests sit down, Zodiac behind his séance table, the others at the centre of the room; the lights dimming to pitch black as they do so. The crystal globe on Zodiac's table brighten as if on queue, shinning on the faces of the quartet, the illuminated heads of Zodiac, Lewis, Rhadini and Chan seemingly floating in the blackness. As Zodiac begins his "supreme demonstration", floating objects hover around the room, and a face, supposedly that of an Egyptian Priestess long dead, appears. She has a message for Chan, from the spirit world, claiming that Paul Essex's death was not from suicide but a weak heart. Rhadini and Lewis aren't impressed by this display, particularly when the spirit then warns Lewis not to marry mind reader Eve Cairo, Lewis' girlfriend and assistant of Rhadini. Lewis and Rhadini rise in anger, denouncing their host as faker and threatening to take him down, and Zodiac, somehow suddenly with gun in hand, orders them off his property. "My servant will see you out" he says as he disappears into the black. As exiled leave, Chan concludes that they must tread carefully in bringing down the pervasive mystic, "to destroy false prophet, must first unmask him before eyes of believers".

That evening, after attending a garden party hosted by Rhadini in which, during a demonstration of her scientifically-verified extra-sensory abilities, Eve senses Zodiac's evil presence, Chan, who was almost struck by a knife he recognizes as the Persian sacrificial knife he saw earlier, decides to pay a late night visit Dr. Zodiac's mansion. As he approaches through the eerie stillness of the night fog, we see the black cat from earlier scuttling across in front of him. As they did on Chan's first visit, Rhadini and Lewis again gatecrash Chan's party, and the three of them enter Zodiac's lair. This time, with the lights turned on, they can see the tricks of the séance room of what they really are, the "levitating" objects operated by switches under the table (look for the skeleton on a string that goes zooming by). Chan also finds the rubber face mask and padded body suit of Dr. Zodiac, from which he deduces that "Zodiac" is actually two other people.

Missing when Essex was found dead was his briefcase containing the manuscript of his book. They recover the manuscript, but find the last page, which contains the solution to the crime depicted in the book, missing. They also unearth the centre of Dr. Zodiac's blackmail web, a fire proof vault that houses the secret files of Zodiac's organized blackmail ring. "What a setup!" whistles Lewis as they scan through cabinets of dossiers containing "all kinds of dope about all kinds of people".

Chan decides to destroy the files, protecting the secret of Paul Essex for his widow, and protecting all the other people whose secrets have fallen into Zodiac's web. He removes all the files from the cabinets and then sets fire to the pile. Rhadini and Lewis, who have been working tirelessly to expose Zodiac's racket since long before Chan arrived on the case, are aghast at the destruction of this important evidence, but "this is best" Chan reasons as the secrets go up in smoke, Chan fulfilling a higher duty than that of his job as a policeman: his duty as a human being.

Since we know that Dr. Zodiac is the one behind it all (even if we don't yet know the truth behind *him*), the film is granted a rare opportunity to delve into the psychology of the murderer. "Dr. Zodiac not ordinary criminal", explains Chan, having brushed up on his psychiatry. "He is man of great ego, with disease known to scientists as pseudologica fantastica" ("is it serious?" a confounded Jimmy asks), "pathological liars and swindlers, suffer from exaggerated fantasy, unleashed vanity and great ambition which robs them of cautious known to saner man".

Few Chan adversaries are really worthy of our favorite detective. They're usually one from an assortment of nondescript suspects, drawn out from the others only at the very end. But with the mysterious "Dr. Zodiac" smokescreen to

CHARLIE CHAN AT TREASURE ISLAND

focus interest on, John Larkin's script is able build up Chan's adversary, making him more dangerous and giving the story a major boost. We rarely see Chan needing to hit the books like this, and the fact alone that Chan must reach beyond his pre-existing knowledge and skill set tells us plenty about what he's up against this time. And from his research and from what he's witnessed, he strikes on two things he thinks may help him take down Zodiac: ego and vanity.

His ego is the big clue to Dr. Zodiac's true identity. It's telling that only adversary the killer considers worthy of his talents, worthy of going up against him, is one that he conjured up himself: the Zodiac persona. It's a fantastic bit of writing, and though we of course don't get to see it, we can just imagine how much enjoyment this joker must be deriving from playing both sides of this game ("Criminal egotist take pleasure in laughing at police" Chan observes). And though his blackmail setup has been discovered and his blackmail files destroyed, our killer could simply discard the now tainted Dr. Zodiac cover, literally and metaphorically shedding the second skin that is the Zodiac mask and padded suit, eluding capture and leaving himself free to assume some other disguise and go about some other racket. "We won't ever see Zodiac with his on whiskers again" Lewis worries.

But he's wrong. Zodiac isn't like most people. Yes, at this point, Zodiac *could* very easy have got off scot free. But if his ego is the big clue to his identity, then his vanity is the big clue to how they can catch him. "Swell head sometimes give police more co-operation than criminal mistake" Chan contends, and they hatch a plan, getting Rhadini to issue a personal challenge to Zodiac...

Which Zodiac accepts, with a return notice written on the back of the elusive last page of the Essex manuscript, no less. And with that the finale is set: a duel between Rhadini and Zodiac before a packed theatre at Rhadini's Temple of Magic, in what is perhaps the most spectacular and dramatic climax of any *Charlie Chan* film.

The night of the challenge arrives. The audience take their seats, abuzz over what might happen, while police cover every door and every exit, ready for anything. Meanwhile, offstage, Rhadini peeks through the curtain fretfully. What if Zodiac doesn't show? What if he *does*? In their seats, the other key players in this drama watch and wait with baited breath.

Rhadini takes the stage. Zodiac has not yet arrived, so Rhadini, ever the showman, endeavors to entertain the audience in the meantime. He brings Chan, Jimmy and Chief Kilvaine up onto the stage; "here's your chance to watch Zodiac up close" he whispers to Chan, as he positions everyone into place. Suddenly the big, broad, enigmatic figure of Dr. Zodiac appears from the wings. A hush blankets of over the theatre as the Doctor smoothly slithers along the aisle and takes his place up on the stage

Rhadini's claim is that any supposedly supernatural feat Zodiac may perform, he can duplicate with old illusionist tricks and misdirection. He offers an example: Levitation. The lights dimmed, Eve lays down on a levitation table and Rhadini waves his wand. The table rises, soaring over the audience to the command of Rhadini's baton. Suddenly, in the cover of darkness and confusion, Zodiac is murdered, slain by an arrow in the heart. Chan removes the dead man's rubber mask to reveal Zodiac's valet, "the Turk".

Kilvaine takes control, simmering down the roused audience and directing them back to their seats. To try to determine who killed the Turk, Chan and co. attempt to piece together what happened by restaging the levitation trick, this time with Jimmy on the table In a re-enactment where anything could happen, it does, and this attempt to restore order results only in more chaos. This time it's Rhadini who is hit, copping a knife to the shoulder while performing the trick, the magician then stretchered off to his dressing room, wounded, but luckily still alive.

But somehow, amidst all this pandemonium, Chan has seen everything he needs to see, and decides to end this show once and for all. This time, it's the real final showdown. Chan brings Eve back up on stage, to call upon her mind reading ability to end this mystery once and for all.

He has the lights, save for the one on Eve's face, turned off. He hypnotizes her and he is now her "control". "Read thoughts in my mind until dominant thought of killer comes to you" he instructs. A thin slit of light illuminates the edge of Chan's face, that otherwise stands completely blanketed in the darkness. Eve closes her eyes and concentrates as he telepathically feeds to her his thoughts; their rhythmic duologue swaying in perfect time with the metronome that ticks back and forth between them.

Eve recites from Chan's mind a rundown the case: of Zodiac's blackmail ring, of Zodiac's culpability in Paul Essex's death, of Zodiac's valet "the Turk", of Zodiac's rival Rhadini, of Zodiac's interfering in the romance between Eve and Lewis. Suddenly... a cloud of confusion begins to seep into Eve's mind. "There is another mind here fighting me, trying to keep your thoughts from me" she cries, now haunted by a new, evil presence. Chan tells her press on. "Continue, please".

"It's Dr. Zodiac! He's not dead!" Eve cries. "He's here in the theatre", as Chan knows he is, and he's is trying to thwart Eve's efforts to read Chan's mind, as Chan knew the would. And now two minds - one good, one evil, but both strong presences - battle for dominance, while between them the troubled Eve struggles in anguish. Chan, mostly in shadow, tries to hold firm, but the mind and the control of the real Zodiac, whose ominous, intruding eyes peer in from the darkness, is also strong, perhaps even stronger. The two begin to grapple for control over Eve Cairo's mind. The battle is on...

BEST MOMENT: [33:02] - There are many to choose from with this one, such as the aforementioned finale with Chan and Zodiac, each in shadow, battling for control over Eve Cairo's mind. But I also like the first display of Eve Cairo's telepathic powers in the earlier scene at the Hawaiian party. Think of it as a preliminary teaser for the main bout between Chan and Zodiac that awaits; this scene establishing and showing off everyone's skills and attributes - Eve's valuable mind reading abilities, Chan's cunning and ingenuity, Rhadini's skill and showmanship, and the mysterious Dr. Zodiacs strength, presence, and evil - and setting everything up for the showdown later. Rhadini and Eve begin performing a demonstration of her abilities for the party, Rhadini placing Eve under hypnosis. "You will seek the mind I name" he commands as the demonstration begins. Tested by members of the audience, Eve first correctly identifies the gold wedding ring of an audience member, reading the ring's engraved inscription, then correctly recites a question that a guest whispers into Rhadini's ear. Chan, believing the Rhadini is somehow signaling messages to Eve, asks Lewis what the trick is, but Lewis insists that it's all genuine. Soon, Chan's turn to test the mind reader comes. He pulls out a card and hands it to Rhadini. Rhadini smiles widely upon viewing Chan's card, which bears an inscription written in Chinese characters. He asks Chan to think of the English translation. Chan does so and from his thoughts Eve is able to read it: "Great happiness follows great pain", proving that she can read not just Rhadini's mind, but "any strong, dominant thought". Chan looks genuinely bewildered, "Most uncanny!"

But just then the thoughts of an unknown, and unwelcome, other appear on Eve's radar. "There's death among us. There's evil here" she shrieks, "someone here is thinking murder". Suddenly, a knife is thrown, narrowly missing Chan.

IN SHORT: Taut and deft. An exhibition of splendor and magnificence. Magic!

CHARLIE CHAN
IN CITY IN DARKNESS (1939)

"Hello. Give me a calamity"
- Marcel Spivak

Sidney Toler (Charlie Chan), **Harold Huber** (Marcel), **Lynn Bari** (Marie Dubon), **Richard Clark** (Tony Madero), **Pedro Dr Cordora** (Antoine), **Dorothy Tree** (Charlotte Ronnell), **C. Henry Gordon** (Prefect of Police), **Douglas Dumbrille** (Petroff), **Noel Madison** (Belescu), **Leo Carroll** (Louis Santelle), **Lon Chaney, Jr.** (Pierre), **Louis Mercier** (Max), **George Davis** (Alex), **Barbara Leonard** (Lola), **Adrienne d' Ambricourt** (Landlady), **Fredrik Vogeding** (Captain).

Director: **Herbert I. Leeds**
Writers: **Robert Ellis** and **Helen Logan** (screenplay),
Gina Kaus and **Ladislaus Fodor** (original play)
Runtime: 75 mins. 20th Century-Fox Film Corp.

Film 20 in the Charlie Chan *series.*

SYNOPSIS: While stranded in Paris on the night of the Munich crisis, Charlie Chan uncovers a plot to smuggle arms to Germany.

Ambition

Until this point, the Charlie Chan films were apt to take place entirely in their own unique world - a world of lush and exotic locations, weird and wonderful characters, strange and incredible sites, and, of course, murder - and in a reality disconnected and unaffected from the goings on of our own, apolitical, with little reference to real people or current events. Only once, briefly, in CHARLIE CHAN AT RENO, for example, is the depression mentioned, and even when Chan visited Berlin in CHARLIE CHAN AT THE OLYMPICS, there was not a swastika to be seen, nor any mention of Hitler or what was going on in Europe at the time. As popular escapist entertainment, the *Charlie Chan* films allowed their audiences to temporarily leave real life behind at the ticket counter, and be taken on a 60-70 minute ride into a different world altogether.

But from the opening of CHARLIE CHAN IN CITY IN DARKNESS, we know that an exception to this rule has surely arrived. Beginning with a narrated prologue chronicling the current turmoil in Europe, we see footage of Germany, Britain, Czechoslovakia and Italy marshalling their respective troops in the "greatest movement of armed forces since the great war", as the fearsome beast of German expansion sets its hungry eyes on Czechoslovakia, threatening "to plunge all Europe into war". We then focus in on Paris, where, by order of the Prefect of Police, every visible light is to be turned out for the entire night, as the city is plunged into darkness as precaution against a possible air raid. While they wait with baited breath for the potential zero hour, citizens clamor for gas masks and provisions, while every plane that flies overhead looked upon with anxiety and fear.

Chan is in Paris, attending a reunion of Military Intelligence veterans, commemorating the 20th anniversary of victory in the First World War while the world teeters on the precipice of the Second. As the champagne, the laughter, and the old war stories flow, Chan solemnly notes that it is "most ironic that reunion to celebrate end of one war finds us waiting zero hour which may start a new one".

We're not in the world of Charlie Chan now; instead he's in *our* world. This time he isn't tracking a murderer hidden among vacationers passing through Honolulu, and for once, people he meet don't gasp in awe and repeat "Charlie Chan" upon hearing his name. Chan, rather unusually, has not made plans for getting out of Paris, his late attempt to obtain passage out of the city showing him and us what's up ahead. "First war profiteer, like early bird, look for big fat worm" Chan remarks when offered an exorbitantly overpriced boat ticket out of Paris, as we're given the sense that something is in the wind and that this is only the beginning.

Previous Chan films, as well as other Hollywood movies of the time, wary of a German boycott or any loss of their International market, took a neutral stance on Hitler and the rise of Nazism in Germany. In CHARLIE CHAN AT THE OLYMPICS, there was no mention of Hitler and not a swastika to be seen, lest depiction be taken as either endorsement or condemnation (though the upraised arm salutes at the Olympic torch was carried to the cauldron at the Opening Ceremony were unavoidable), while the local law enforcement depicted was more Kaiser than Gestapo. Chan's only comment on it all was that "would be greatest blessing if all war fought with machinery instead of human beings". This time, however, two years later, we have a Chan film not only willing to say something, but wanting to say something. Just as the villains of CHARLIE CHAN IN CITY IN DARKNESS, a ring of gunrunners smuggling munitions, have disguised their contraband artillery as crates of fruit, so too is this film really something else, a propaganda piece of sorts, delivered as a *Charlie Chan* movie, the writers (Gina Kaus and Ladislaus Fodor wrote the original play, while veteran Chan scribes Robert Ellis and Helen Logan adapted it into a Chan film for the screen) and the studio taking the opportunity to make a big statement: that contrary to what you may or may not have heard, war is most certainly on its way. From this standpoint alone, CHARLIE CHAN IN CITY IN DARKNESS is certainly the most ambitious film of the series. But is it any good?

Sadly, not especially. Firstly, the film probably should have been titled "Marcel Spivak in City in Darkness", for the loud, broad, hammy comedy of Harold Huber's inept Romanian Policeman character, who doesn't so much dominate proceedings as take them over completely with his incessant hollering and howling and his endless blustering and flustering. Perhaps the director felt, given the serious nature of the subject, and the lack of much humor involved beyond some sly political satire, that he needed to add more overt comedy wherever he could, to make this otherwise ominous political piece more palatable for audiences. Whatever the case, Marcel is allowed to completely run amok, or rather, completely stumble and bumble ineptly amok.

It's a loud and one-note performance, insufferable, deafening, and void of any nuance or subtly or contemplation or restraint. Every gesture is exaggerated, every syllable of speech shouted. He's never just scared, he's petrified; never just in need, but desperate; never just elated, but utterly ecstatic; and never just depressed, but utterly despondent. It's all just too much, and its obnoxiousness is compounded by the fact that he is in nearly every minute of the movie, and is front and centre for nearly every minute of the movie. Broad comedy has never been so high on the broad, or so low on the comedy. With frantic, but forced and misplaced energy, he just spins on his wheels, going everywhere but getting nowhere. As premature to cry surrender as he is to declare victory, he seems to know only elation and despair with nothing in between. "How can I explain to my papa that the murderer slipped through my fingers?" he mopes inconsolably, before moments later declaring "we have uncovered the greatest spy ring in France. We are heroes". "Come on, Mr. Chan" he cries triumphantly, "Let us go". "Go where?" Chan asks, his way of pointing out that they have no further leads. "I don't know" Marcel frowns weakly as he twigs.

"Always I have wanted to be a detective" Marcel says early on, trying to appeal to Chan's sympathies and get his assistance, "but Papa keeps me only as his secretary". But with the Prefect tied up dealing with the fallout of the blackout, the murder investigation is left to Marcel. "Tonight is my one big chance to show what I can do" he says. And show what he can do he does.

Toler as Chan actually makes for a very effective deadpan straight man - "excellent deduction. Am certain worthy parent would be proud" he remarks when Marcel points out the obvious, that a window is broken (and watch as he subtly peers over Marcel's shoulder as Marcel makes notes) - but it's a waste of a character, and an actor, who we know are so much more. Toler is so subdued at times it's as if he was just content to go along for the ride on this one. Though despite this almost support player status, Chan still manages to do all the detective work. Every discovery, every deduction, every decision of what to next, is made by Chan, while the useless Marcel hollers and howls. This film may put Chan in the passenger seat, but somehow he still does all the driving.

But it would be unfair to place the entire brunt on Huber and the Marcel character. In truth, the premise, a one-night runaround about Paris really isn't suited to the meretricious, methodical Chan, nor vice versa, the story uninvolving enough without a lead character of profound detachment compounding the situation. That the story wasn't originally written with Charlie Chan in mind is evident, not just from the opening credits. The best scenes are actually when Huber and Toler aren't on screen (and the best acting by those who have no or limited interaction with them), when the straight dramas of the characters affected by the blackout and the oncoming war are allowed to play out, this "serious relief" a much welcome respite from the deluge of deafening "comedy".

Such as the goings on at the *Hotel Des Voyagours*, where a guest who wont sign the register hides away in his upstairs room. Peeking outside from behind the curtain, he's hiding out after having been false accused of some crime, waiting for his wife, who has raised the money to buy him a forged passport, only for the unscrupulous forger to have boosted his asking price in light of the looming crisis.

And then there's Antoine, the crippled valet whose young son Philippe has been called up to the Army. In his oversize uniform and carrying a backpack that almost as big as he is, the baby-faced Philippe seems awfully young for war, though he is 19. "I wasn't much more than that when I went to the trenches" his father beams with pride. That he may end up crippled like his father doesn't faze the young man: "It's a chance a solider must take" he says with sureness. Antoine's master, the cynical Petroff, wonders why the French should aid Czechoslovakia. "Because they're fighting for liberty and ours may be next" Antoine, a principled spokesman for the main message of the whole film, explains. "Liberty? The revolution taught you to bray like a lot of jackasses about liberty - you've been doing it ever since" the tetchy Petroff dismissively snorts.

The wealthy exporter Petroff is later revealed to another "war profiteer", working with a spy ring in a plot to smuggle munitions out of France and into the hands of the Germans. The spy ring's plans are complicated first by the blackout, then by the sudden murder of Petroff, who is killed while organizing last-minute clearance papers for the munitions, and it's with Petroff's murder that Chan and Marcel are drawn into the case.

Eventually all the players - three unlucky burglars who broke into Petroff's house at the wrong time, the husband and wife trying to get out of Paris, the forger, Petroff's business partner, and Petroff's butler Antoine - are brought to the Prefect's office, though Marcel has no idea what to do with them. Mercifully for him (and us), Chan arrives. "Most interesting assembly" he says, which is rather a generous description of this ensemble. He begins airing out the dirty laundry, laying out the facts, and drawing out the truth from the various suspects, as we've seen him do so many times before, but this time, just as we think he's about name the killer, the murder mystery has to be put on hold, when the deafening noise of what is taken to be an air raid suddenly crashes the party; the real world intruding on the world of Charlie Chan yet again. The sound is actually that of a patrol of French Army planes passing overhead, but as everyone drops everything to duck and cover, we see the impact that warfare has on all other facets of life, the way that war halts everything else, even *Charlie Chan* movies (as World War II, of course, will later do). Using deconstruction to make its statement, it's moments like this that somewhat redeem the film.

But there's little detective work, little focus, and ultimately little to maintain interest, and long before the end, when gun runners' scheme is undone by bad luck rather than bad play, you won't care who has done what or why.

CHARLIE CHAN IN CITY IN DARKNESS is widely regarded as the least of the Twentieth Century-Fox *Charlie Chan* pictures. The direction, as well as letting Marcel run amok, doesn't help alleviate the story flaws, and it's all a rather stodgy, lifeless, and mediocre 75 mins. Yes, it's ambitious, yes, it's trying something different, and yes, it has a worthwhile point to make, but that doesn't mean we can't find much of it disappointing.

As the film began with the reunion of WWI veterans around a table toasting that victory, so it ends with Chan, the Prefect of Police and friends around a table toasting the success of this case (albeit this time over morning coffee rather than afternoon champagne), with Chan and Marcel having rounded up "one of the most dangerous spy rings that ever threatened the safety of France". But there is still the matter of the murder of Petroff to clear up. The murderer is revealed to be one of the parties present at the celebratory table, though this time the circumstances are different here than in any other Chan film, in that the murder was committed not for profit or revenge, and not out of jealousy, greed or spite, but for country and for freedom, for love, honor and duty. Chan agrees that in this instance "murder" is the wrong word for what was clearly done "in defense of country".

The "killer" stands up straight and tall and admits to everything. He tells of how he couldn't bear the thought of the smuggled arms being used against French soldiers, but he

131

offers all this as an explanation, not an excuse. Slightly nervous about what might become of him, but defiant, stanch, and true, he is prepared to take what comes, even if that means the firing squad. He has faced death before.

But has he ever faced, The Prefect of Police wonders, "a general, pinning a Croix de Guerre on your chest and kissing you on both checks", and rather than being handcuffed by some anonymous officer and lead off to where all other *Charlie Chan* killers are escorted (i.e. off screen), it seems the killer of this piece is also the hero of this piece.

The jubilation continues when a telegram arrives for the Prefect, and it is here that we come to the film's powerful moment: Chan's closing line. The Prefect smiles as he scans the telegram, announcing that it bears the "good news" that French Prime Minister Edouard Daladier and British Prime Minister Neville Chamberlain have been invited by Hitler to Munich for a conference. The others, elated and relieved, take this news to mean that there will be no war after all. But Chan, ever prophetic, is less convinced, warning "beware of spider who invite fly to parlor".

BEST MOMENT: [73:51] - The aforementioned closing line, perhaps, given the context, Chan's most potent and meaningful aphorism ever.

IN SHORT: A bombastic performance from Harold Huber and an unengaging narrative make this topical Chan a rare misfire.

CHARLIE CHAN IN PANAMA (1940)

"In Panama, walls equipped with eyes as well as ears"
- Charlie Chan

Sidney Toler (Charlie Chan), **Sen Yung** (Number Two Son Jimmy), **Jean Rogers** (Kathi Lenesch), **Lionel Atwill** (Cliveden Compton), **Mary Nash** (Miss Finch), **Kane Richmond** (Richard Cabot), **Chris-Pin Martin** (Montero), **Lionel Royce** (Dr. Rudolph Grosser), **Helen Ericson** (Stewardess), **Jack La Rue** (Manolo), **Edwin Stanley** (Governor Webster), **Don Douglas** (Captain Lewis), **Frank Puglia** (Achmed Halide), **Addison Richards** (Godley), **Edward Keane** (Dr. Fredericks).

Director: **Norman Foster**
Screenplay: **John Larkin** and **Lester Ziffren**
Runtime: 67 mins. 20th Century-Fox Film Corp.

Film 21 in the Charlie Chan *series.*

SYNOPSIS: Working undercover for the U.S. Government, Charlie Chan must save the Panama Canal from a master saboteur.

Suspicion

The Charlie Chan series enters the 1940s with this vibrant, exciting, and topical - if not entirely typical - outing. "Charlie Chan defies the enemies of America" proclaimed the trailer for this lively, rollicking adventure, as Chan, working undercover on loan to the U.S. Government, must sift through a regular "City of Spies" to find the master saboteur who has set their sights on the Panama Canal in what must surely rank as one of the best films of the series.

We open on a Military Reservation in the Panama Canal Zone. As a warship passes by, we focus in on a signpost warning that "taking photographs in this area (is) absolutely forbidden" by order of the U.S. Army.

Two military policemen, vigilant enforcers of the reservation's strict security restrictions, creep up toward a scruffy looking fisherman angling idly on the edge of the pier. They encroach in on him slowly, steadily, incrementally, hiding behind some crates as they watch him, waiting. What these two MPs could possibly want with the seemingly languid and dozy figure that sits before us we're not immediately certain, but we very soon get our answer. This unlikely individual is a spy. Unaware that he is now under surveillance, the "fisherman" casually lifts up his straw hat and with slow, cautious movements pulls out from his shabby fishing basket a camera with a telephoto lens, expensive equipment for such a disheveled laborer, which he then uses to take some covert snaps of the nearby warship's seaplane catapult in action. His reconnaissance work done, he slyly slips the camera back in his basket, concealing it among his other catch for the day. But as sly and as subtle and as crafty and as cunning in his movements as he may be, his actions have been witnessed by the two MPs, who, seeing all they need to see, move in. The spy rises and turns to leave, only to find himself face to face with the looming MPs, but rather that face arrest, he tries to make a run for it, diving for the water as his pursuers open fire.

"Why are the shooting at him? The poor man was only fishing" Miss Jennie Finch, a prim and proper lady of about 50, asks two of her fellow travelers, having observed this activity from the other side of the pier. "With a camera equipped a telephoto lens" one of them observes. Miss Finch seems surprised and disappointed - "*that* dirty old fisherman a spy?" she says, as if rather disillusioned - but while this vacationing Chicago school teacher, who perhaps expected her spies to be "handsome, suave men of the world", may not be impressed by "the dirty old fisherman" being a spy, what it tells us is that anyone, *anyone*, could be a secret agent.

Anyone, including, quite possibly, Miss Finch's two present companions, Emil Manolo, and Cliveden Compton, who, both knowing this, trade thinly veiled allusions to each other over what they've just witnessed. "You two make me nervous, as if you suddenly didn't trust each other" Miss Finch observes of them. Manolo, a local, shrugs it off as nothing personal. "It's the atmosphere of this place" he says, as he explains that the canal "draws agents of all countries here". "A city of spies" is how he rather dashingly describes it, and the Englishman Compton nods in agreement, warning Miss Finch that she's now "in dangerous territory". "At least we're getting off to an exciting start" she remarks, and it's indeed one of the finest set-ups to a Chan film, capturing the atmosphere and tension and danger that hangs in the air.

Waiting to board their connecting seaplane for their flight across the canal to Panama City, they're soon joined by a Mr. Godley, who Manolo seems put out to see, Compton delighted, and Miss Finch curious. Godley, as we'll soon learn, is a US government agent, in pursuit of the notorious secret agent and saboteur known only as "Ryner", who, as we'll soon learn, is one of the six other passengers now boarding the seaplane.

The three we've already met, Panama City nightclub owner Manolo, English novelist Compton, and Chicago school teacher Miss Finch, are soon joined on the plane by Dr. Rudolph Grosser, an Austrian scientist who specializes in tropical diseases, Kathi Lenesch, a cabaret singer who has just obtained a job working at Manolo's club, and Achmed Halide, a shady local tobacconist. All are deftly implicated in one way or another, and each will at one point be declared by Jimmy Chan to be Ryner ("I've got it, Pop! He/she is Ryner"). In fact, any of them could be Ryner. Any of them could be a spy working for or against Ryner. But one of them, whichever one slipped the poison cigarettes into Godley's coat pocket while they were all on the seaplane, is the vicious and elusive foreign saboteur, who now has their sights set on that most vital of American naval strategic assets , the Panama Canal. And as seen at the beginning, this is Panama, and everyone is a suspect.

And everyone, it seems, is up to something suspicious. Why does Manolo want Kathi to "get acquainted" with US Government engineer Cabot and find out all she can about him? And what does he have over her? Is Dr. Grosser, in his "delicate experiment", infecting his rats with bubonic plague, in a plot to unleash them onto the fleet? Is Cliveden Compton really English, or merely playing a part? Did Achmed Halide, who is a tobacconist after all, have something to do with the poison cigarette? And why is he always skulking around where trouble is to be found? And why is he so afraid of Dr. Grosser's work? And what are he and Compton *really* up to? "Isn't this exciting?" Miss Finch again asks joyfully, as the seaplane takes off for Panama City.

Since we know that the murderer is Ryner (whoever Ryner may be), master saboteur and enemy of America, the script isn't saddled with the burden of having to provide each of its suspects with individual motives for the murder of Godley, and instead is free simply to cast suspicion. We know the whydunit, the question is whodunit. There is loads of misdirection and all the suspects play their parts well.

Having painted a backdrop in which suspicion and distrust can thrive, and populated it with appropriately shady characters, it's time now to introduce our heroes and kill off our victim. Unusually, Chan is wearing a different hat in this one, working this time not for the Honolulu Police, but instead on loan to Army Intelligence, undercover as Panama hat store proprietor Fu Yuen. Indeed nothing is what it seems in Panama! Godley enters the store to make contact with our favorite detec.., um, intelligence operative. Speaking in cautious, hushed whispers, while acting out the roles of storeowner and customer - for "in Panama, walls equipped with eyes as well as ears" - they discuss the tip regarding an attempted attack on the canal set for tomorrow night, Chan noting that he has noticed a large increase in the number of secret agents in the city. Godley also brings news that the notorious Ryner, responsible for several recent successful sabotages, is now in Panama City. "Ryner's Brilliant. Yet a cold blooded killer" Godley exclaims, explaining that no one has any idea as to Ryner's identity, or what he or she even looks like.

"You can't be too careful" is Godley's philosophy, as he and Chan exchange passphrases upon making contact, but even he's not careful enough to escape the wrath of Ryner. As he's about to divulge to Chan the one clue he has uncovered in regards to Ryder's identify, Godley lights a cigarette from his coat, and, with just one puff, keels over, dying instantly.

How unusual it is for the murder to take place before Chan's very eyes, with Chan as the only witness and, for a few moments at least, the chief suspect. But that he's hauled off by the police isn't as bad as it might otherwise sound, for though the arresting officer is proud of his haul, and though a crowd of curious onlookers have been drawn to the scene upon hearing the words "murder" and/or "spy", the arrest has the feel of official procedure just-going-though-the-motions about it, Chan even permitted to grab his hat as he is promptly, yet casually, escorted to jail. This is just another day in Panama.

But how unusual it is that our two heroes should meet up in a police holding cell, with Jimmy having also been arrested under suspicion of being a spy (though in his case he was caught innocently, if dimwittedly, stopping to take some photos of the battleships when the ocean liner he was working as a steward on during his college vacation stopped in Panama). Aware of Chan's business in Panama, Jimmy remarks that "working on a case together is just like old times". Chan wasn't aware of the "current collaboration", but Jimmy assures his Pop "you'll be proud of me yet".

The reason for this influx of spies from all sides, the reason for this heighten level of security and angst, the reason for the murder of Godley, the reason for Chan's call up to the service, the reason for Ryner's presence in Panama, and the object of everyone's fixation: The Panama Canal, and an expected sabotage attempt on one of the locks. And the clock is ticking. For in just 18 hours, the U.S. Naval Fleet's full compliment of warships is due to pass though the canal to get back to its battle stations in the Pacific. It's suspected that Ryner will strike at that time for maximum impact, trapping the fleet in the canal, the battleships "caught like fish in trap".

Time is of the essence, and the consequences will be devastating if Ryner isn't stopped. The Governor assures Chan that he has the "full resources of Military Intelligence" at his disposal, but Chan decides it would be best if he and Jimmy continue to work undercover. Both Toler and particularly Yung (back after being absent from CITY IN DARKNESS) are in great form as Chan and Jimmy encounter the suspects and sneak around their offices and hotel rooms in the middle of night. With the only clue to Ryner's identity being that the saboteur was among the passengers who arrived in Panama City on the seaplane with Godley, Chan and Jimmy have their work cut out for them as they comb through the sextet of suspects, uncovering many of their secrets and lies and facades as they try to deduce which of them is Godley's killer. But it's by no means easy going. They get caught up in another spy scare later at Manolo's club and are almost arrested for a second time, needing to blow their cover to in order save themselves, and are later enclosed in a tomb by the crafty Ryner; trapped with just hours to go before the fleet is due to reach the canal, with seemingly no way to get out or send word.

On the second viewing, when you know the score, the murderer's performance is a joy. Watch this one again, when you know everyone's allegiances and alliances, and watch as everything takes on new meaning. Suddenly curious glances become investigative inspections, innocent enquires become probing questions, and the idle pleasantries of polite acquaintances become the shrewd conniving of secret confederates. The screenplay, by John Larkin and Lester Ziffren, is dashing and exciting and joyfully constructed, with every secret uncovered by Chan and Jimmy, and every revelation made about one of the suspects, bringing what's come before it into greater focus, and shining just a little more light on the dark picture of Ryner. If it has one or two logical flaws, particularly with the standoff at the finale, it all moves along so swiftly and so slickly, so spryly and so cleverly, and with such aplomb, that you'll either not notice or not care.

Norman Foster, the director responsible for re-shaping the series for the Sidney Toler Era with CHARLIE CHAN IN RENO and CHARLIE CHAN AT TREASURE ISLAND returns to helm this perhaps the most sumptuous film of the series. Aided by the cinematography of Virgil Miller, set decoration by Thomas Little, and art direction by Richard Day and Chester Gore, this is a cornucopia of striking sets and scenic locations. During the day the streets, packed with stores and markets and fruit stands and weave baskets, are a hive of activity and bustle as people go about their daily business. At night, as the crickets come out to chirp, you can feel the heat and almost touch the lush foliage. Manolo's nightclub, a large, lofty, two story affair packed with rowdy sailors and dolled-up women who try to withstand them, buzzes with music and carousing. The local cemetery is a virtual jungle of tombstones and overgrowth. The Egyptian tomb of Achmed Halide, which Ryner has been using to store explosives, is richly loaded candles and cobwebs. On every street corner, there's a guitar player, and in every room, a ceiling fan on full tilt. The streets and alleys, the hotels and military bases, the swanky nightclubs and seedy bars, the clean, modern government offices and the grimy, rundown police holding cells, the rickety seaplane that brings Ryner and the other suspects to Panama, and the magnificent Miraflores Lock Power Station they might not ever leave alive: There won't be a Chan film that will have sets and locations, both exterior and interior, of this quality and quantity again.

Interestingly, just as "Charlie Chan at the Ringside" was, after Warner Oland walked off the set, re-worked into MR.

MOTO'S GAMBLE starring Peter Lorre, so too was this story, original slated to be a Moto film, re-assigned as a Charlie Chan picture. In both cases this fact is somewhat evident. MR. MOTO'S GAMBLE of course, co-stars Keye Luke as Lee Chan, and has some Chan-esque dialogue and other features more associated with the Chan series, while CHARLIE CHAN IN PANAMA, opening with Chan working undercover as a hat store proprietor, has a few features atypical in a Chan film, the final gambit employing a more aggressive, calculating Moto-esque type of cunning, rather than the pristine and candid Chan-esque brand we're more accustomed to. And yet, as Chan, in last ditch effort to wrangle a confession from Ryner, seals himself and his suspects in the lock power station facility, where it's believed that a bomb has somewhere been planted by the saboteur, and as the time continues to ticks forward, the bomb due to go off at any second, and as panic sets in among his captors, who, while Chan blocks the only exit, contemplate mutiny, we're in for the most tense, most thrilling and most nerve-racking finish to what is one of the most wonderfully written, wonderfully cast, wonderfully designed and wonderfully directed Chan films.

Having saved the canal, Chan and Jimmy watch on as the U.S. Naval fleet passes safely through. "A great sight" beams Jimmy, as we see the fleet of battleships in full flight and in full might. We then close on a two-shot of Charlie Chan and Number Two Son Jimmy, as Chan remarks that "Intelligent defense of nation best guarantee for years of peace".

BEST MOMENT: [1:01:38] - The finale. The fleet, already on the move and unable to be halted, are due to pass though the Miraflores lock at 10pm, and with the bomb set to go off some time around then, time is running out.

Chan has the suspects meet them at the lock's powerhouse facility. The Governor has order a sweep of the lock, but despite his men's best efforts, we're told that they've been unable to find the bomb (we know it's been planted near the drinking fountain). With that an evacuation is ordered, and everyone in the facility - military personnel, officials, lock workers, etc - hurries of the exit.

But just as everyone else has made it out, Chan seals himself and the remaining suspects in the room. "Must ask present group to remain" he says, as if they have any say in the matter, as he stands over the door, gun in hand. Announcing that one of them is the saboteur Ryder, he takes this impromptu opportunity to question each of them, trying to force a confession as his captives become more and more overcome with fear. Everyone knows the bomb will go off soon, though only Ryner knows exactly when. Only Ryner knows where the bomb is and the exact moment when it will go off. "Only Ryner can safe own life and others".

"Supposed he's the kind who's willing to die?" Miss Finch wails. Chan has considered this, but wonders if the killer can, as the hands of the clock tick forward, marching toward the zero point, "wait, minute by minute, second by second?"; Chan's rationale being that the only thing more nerve wracking right now than not knowing when the bomb will go off is *knowing* when the bomb will go off.

"You fool! You'll die too!" one of imprisoned exclaims. "Am willing to assume risk, to assist fleet of favorite nation" Chan replies. The coolness in his direct and forthright explanation of what he's doing, then his steel nerve as panic sets in among his captives and the three men among his prisoners contemplate taking matters into their own hands, shine through. "Stay where you are" he demands as the men make to advance, his gun still pointed toward them. But Chan not the only one who is armed, as Ryner is finally revealed...

IN SHORT: Toler and Yung, surrounded by a good cast of suspects, are in fine form in this sleek, vibrant, sumptuous adventure / mystery from director Norman Foster.

CHARLIE CHAN'S MURDER CRUISE (1940)

"To think without speaking is to shoot without aiming"
- Charlie Chan

Sidney Toler (Charlie Chan), **Sen Yung** (Number Two Son Jimmy), **Marjorie Weaver** (Paula Drake), **Lionel Atwill** (Dr. Suderman), **Robert Lowery** (Dick Kenyon), **Don Beddoe** (Frederick Ross), **Leo Carroll** (Professor Gordon), **Cora Witherspoon** (Susie Watson), **Kay Linaker** (Mrs. Pendleton), **Harlan Briggs** (Coroner), **Charles Middleton** (Mr. Walters), **Claire Du Brey** (Mrs. Walters), **Leonard Mudie** (Gerald Pendleton), **James Burke** (Wilkie), **Richard Keene** (Buttons), **Layne Tom, Jr.** (Number Seven Son Willie), **Montague Shaw** (Inspector Duff).

Director: **Eugene Forde**
Screenplay: **Robertson White** and **Lester Ziffren**
Runtime: 75 mins. 20th Century-Fox Film Corp.

Film 22 in the Charlie Chan *series. A remake of CHARLIE CHAN CARRIES ON.*

SYNOPSIS: When a Scotland Yard Investigator pursuing a murderer on an around-the-world cruise is himself murdered, it falls to Charlie Chan to carry on the investigation.

Appeal

Chan, a bunch of red herrings, and the murderer board a boat. Again. Son stows away on board to offer Pop "assistance". Again. Chan is out to find the murderer of an old friend. Again. A former spouse, now "blinded", is wheeled in to identify the killer by their voice. Again. Chan points the finger at an innocent in order to smoke out the real killer. Again. Misleading reaction shots of people looking guilty even though they have absolutely nothing to hide. Again. The lights go out. *Again.*

Actually a remake of CHARLIE CHAN CARRIES ON, but though that film may be long lost, one still can't help but feel that we've seen this all before. A key plot point to the killer's *modus operandi* is lifted straight from CHARLIE CHAN IN PARIS, the gag of Chan feigning not to know his captured stowaway son is recycled from CHARLIE CHAN AT THE RACE TRACK, and even the film's title card - with the palm trees of Hawaii - and accompanying music are the same as that of CHARLIE CHAN IN HONOLULU.

For some, this will seem a tedious rehash creatively lacking. For others, a glorious greatest hits package. But after two topical outings, the ambitious misfire that was CHARLIE CHAN IN CITY IN DARKNESS, and the wonderful, but atypical CHARLIE CHAN IN PANAMA, it's perhaps not surprising that the filmmakers would elect to return to familiar waters in an attempt recapture the Charlie Chan magic. Or was it simply because of a lack of new material?

Whatever the case, it begins wonderfully. Inspector Duff of Scotland Yard arrives in Honolulu and calls in on Chan at Chan's office. He meets two of Chan's sons, Jimmy and Willie, who he describes as "carbon copies of my own back home" (a clever touch that establishes that he a father, of children who will never see him again and will feel the loss when he is slain a few minutes later). Getting down to business, he tells Chan of a killer that he had been recently pursuing: A strangler, one so clever that the Inspector has "travelled the world all over with him, or her, and learnt practically nothing". "The fox is running with the hounds this time" he says, explaining that the strangler is one of 10 passengers of an around-the-world cruise organized by a Dr. Suderman, and that Duff has been travelling with the cruise incognito trying to work out which, but has so far turned up nothing. And with Honolulu the last stop before the cruise reaches its finish in San Francisco, he's running out of time to catch his man. Chan agrees to help and the two of them make plans to pay the cruise members a visit at their hotel, to see if they can somehow smoke the killer out. Chan leaves Duff alone in his office for a moment (big mistake) whilst he goes to fill his Chief in on the case. He and the Chief return to find the good Inspector laid out on the floor, strangled. Without a moment's hesitation, Chan requests that his boss assign him to the case. *"Inspector very old and honored friend. Vicious attack in own office bitter challenge to friendship. Challenge will not go unanswered"*.

And with that, the stage is set for a cracking Chan mystery. We know that the killer is clever, having eluded capture and concealed his identify from a capable detective while travelling right beside him. We know that he is dangerous and that Chan is now walking into danger; the killer having already slain one pursuer and Chan stepping straight into that dead man's shoes. We know that this is in some way personal for Chan; the killer having murdered his old friend, in Chan's office no less. And we know the clock is ticking, with Chan having only until the cruise reaches its San Francisco destination to figure out which of the passengers is the killer, before they're all free to "scatter to the four corners of the world". The writers have pithily streamlined the original *Charlie Chan Carries On* story, condensing the non-Chan first half of the investigation into Inspector Duff's opening monologue, while retaining the potent elements of the Earl Derr Biggers material and elevating the setup to something above the norm.

From here though, it's not quite as successful. Chan makes alone the trip he and Duff had planed, venturing to the hotel to meet the passengers, who range from very annoying to marginally less annoying. The first of the cruise members he meets, archaeologist Professor Gordon, is fed up of the rest; "I'm worn out of looking at the same old faces" he sighs, and we'll soon understand how he feels. He and Chan enter the hotel to the news that another member of the party, a "Mr. Kenyon" has also been strangled. "He and his nephew are on the cruise" Gordon gasps. "How do you know it was uncle and not nephew (who was murdered)?" Chan wonders, interested in the Professor's slip of tongue.

The loose tongues and slips of tongues continue. Chan doesn't have to go far to meet the rest of party; they all come to him. Nor does he have to apply the most probing or crafty of interview or interrogation techniques in order to get them to talk; they're all seemingly desperate to have their say. Aside from the latest victim's nephew, Dick Kenyon, and the director of the cruise, the tedious Dr. Sudermen (who never stops trying to salvage his business, even after multiple murders have been committed), we also have the piercing screams of the shrieking Susie Watson, who talks loudly, natters constantly, and says absolutely nothing ("well he looked like... his eyes... well he sort of... no, I couldn't swear to it" is her concise description of the assailant) and her secretary, and Dick Kenyon's fiancé, Paula Drake. They're followed by the laidback playboy Frederick Ross, who calmly rattles off his vital statistics for Chan's notebook: "Weight: 168 pounds, height: five foot ten, and a bit to 35".

Two walking corpse, a Mr. and Mrs. Walters, come in next, to offer testimony no one asked for, with the kooky, morbid Mrs. Walters claiming that she earlier overheard Dick and his uncle having a quarrel in which the elder Kenyon referred the younger's fiancé Paula as an "adventuress". Dick's made-up-on-the-spot explanation for this, a rather lame alibi about his uncle reading a mystery story when he "jokingly" make the remark about Paula, does more to confirm than refute Mrs. Walters claim.

Last and least is the highly strung Mr. Pendleton, occupant of the room that Kenyon was strangled in; news he seems to find terribly nerve-racking but not terribly surprising, his hand instinctively moving to his own neck upon hearing the word "strangled", and news that has him desperate to pack his bags and check in to another hotel. "I won't stay here another minute. I'm a sick man, under a doctor's care" he insists. The one guy less than keen to talk (rendering him the most sympathetic of the group), he seems genuinely petrified, in a way that lets on that he knows more than he lets on (which sets him apart from the others, who all clearly know far *less* than they let on).

If any of them could keep their mouths shut they all might just avoid suspicion, but it seems they're all keen to give what plus a pair of pennies would be their two cents worth. As Chan himself puts it, "to speak without thinking is to shoot without aiming".

And it's indeed by speaking without thinking that the killer overplays their part, saying too much and providing Chan with a big clue that he or she is not what they claim to be. But since only 44 minutes have past by this point, Chan can't zero in on this suspect just yet, and instead has to whittle away some time judging a hobby horse race, allowing for another death or two to take place in the interim, first of the panicky Pendleton, then of Ross. And here the story, like the cruise, sort of just floats along, waiting to arrive at its endpoint, a missing leather shoelace and an intercepted telegram from the late Pendleton to his wife proving rather uninvolving clues. "Truth like oil - will in time rise to service" says Chan, but it seems to take a while.

Finally the boat reaches San Francisco, but this expedition isn't quite over yet, as Chan drags those still alive to the morgue for what is supposedly Ross' inquest but is actually Chan's denouement. Here he does the "killer now in this room" bit, then the "blinded ex-wife who can only identify her former husband by their voice" bit, then the "pointing the finger at an innocent in order to smoke the real killer out" bit, then the "capturing the killer as he tries to kill again" bit (though why the killer doesn't wait for another, less teeming-with-police, opportunity to try to off his ex-wife I'm not sure. "He's mad" isn't a great explanation as far as explanations go, especially since he was cool enough in his thinking to pull off his other murders without discovery, but I suspect it's the best explanation we're going to get), and then, finally, the "account of how he suspected that so-and-so was the killer the whole time" bit. We even have the lights go out at one point amidst all that the aforementioned pandemonium. I'm all for each and every one of these tropes, but somehow here, all of them strung together one after another here in the morgue, it all feels cluttered and convoluted rather than clever. And so very, very familiar.

But then, imagine yourself a movie goer in 1940. Infact, imagine yourself not only one movie goer, but an entire audience of movie goer, each of whom has handed over their 15c to see a double feature, each of whom has their own different tastes and contrasting cravings, and each of whom must come away from their night at the movies satisfied and wanting to come back again for the next *Charlie Chan* picture. There's nothing wrong with mass entertainment, and in the *Charlie Chan* film, mass entertainment has rarely been as entertaining, nor as mass.

There's mystery. There's intrigue. There's romance. There's comedy. There's action and gunplay. There's travel and adventure. And while individual Chan films may not have always hit every bullseye of each of these targets - sometimes the comedy doesn't catch fire, or occasionally the mystery mightn't engage us as much as usual - they nearly always served up hearty doses of most of what fans came back again and again for. And while we can usually rely on Chan films to be a little more inventive and imaginative than CHARLIE CHAN'S MURDER CRUISE, what we do have here is yet another grand and highly entertaining and pleasing 75 minutes, which one suspects that for Chan fans once again delivered everything they hoped it would.

BEST MOMENT: [47:42] - Chan sees Paula alone on the boat deck, looking out at the ocean under the moonlight. He approaches and they discuss her fiancé and his poor explanation regarding the quarrel he had with his uncle shortly before he died. Paula wonders if she should be worried about this. "One cloud does not make storm, nor one falsehood criminal" Chan answers. Chan asks Paula if she still trust Dick. "I want to very much", she answers. "Then do" Chan says, "but trust must be shared. Let young man know what is in heart". When asked if *he* believes Dick is innocent, Chan offers some interesting personal insight. "Unfortunate profession make detective suspect innocent with guilty", he says matter-of-factly but also somewhat introspectively. "But not so with lovers" he adds hopefully, with an optimism that he hopes is contagious as he tries to persuade her not to lose faith. He succeeds and her mood brightens.

It's a scene more commonly found in an Oland film than in a Toler one, though in any incarnation Chan has always been a matchmaker, gently, not abrasively or forcefully, steering couples through the choppy waters and to their happily-ever-after destination.

IN SHORT: All too familiar Chan starts off well, but then treads water until a noisy, cluttered finale.

CHARLIE CHAN
AT THE WAX MUSEUM (1940)

"Justice can be brought to dead man"
- Charlie Chan

Sidney Toler (Charlie Chan), **Sen Yung** (Number Two Son Jimmy),
C. Henry Gordon (Dr. Cream), **Marc Lawrence** (Steve McBirney),
Joan Valerie (Lily Latimer), **Marguerite Chapman** (Mary Bolton),
Ted Osborn (Tom Agnew), **Michal Visaroff** (Dr. Otto Von Brom),
Hilda Vaughn (Mrs. Rocke), **Charles Wagenheim** (Willie Fern),
Archie Twitchell (Carter Lane), **Edward Marr** (Grenock), **Joe King**
(Inspector O'Matthews), **Harold Goodwin** (Edwards).

Director: **Lynn Shores**
Screenplay: **John Larkin**
Runtime: 63 mins. 20th Century-Fox Film Corp.

Film 23 in the Charlie Chan *series.*

SYNOPSIS: When a murderer, convicted on evidence given by
Charlie Chan and sentenced to death, flees police custody, he
lures Chan to a wax museum of crime with hopes of exacting
revenge.

Reputation

One day we will die. But long after we are gone, our name
and reputation will continue to live on, a fact evident by the
crop of famous detectives and notorious killers whose images
have been immortalized in wax figure form at Dr. Cream's
bizarre wax museum of crime. Mrs. Rocke, the widow of Joe
Rocke, knows this. Though her husband was long ago
convicted of murder and executed, his case is still widely
debated, and she, adamant that he was framed and wrongfully
convicted, and weary of hearing the vicious lies spoken about
him, is determined to clear his name. Charlie Chan, who also

believes that Rocke may be innocent, knows this too, hence his assertion that "justice can be brought to dead man".

But it's not only the reputations of the dead that are of concern. We're told that the "cops never bother" Dr. Cream, for he was once known as the "best facial surgeon in the country", and it's that good name and standing that enables him to carry out his racket, performing facial surgery operations for criminals, without any interference from police (he even tries to make use of his reputation later on, "My work, purely educational, endorsed by schools and colleges" he boasts, trying to dupe the increasingly suspicious Chan). And everybody knows, or at least should know, who gangster and killer Steve McBirney is: "Don't you recognize Steve McBirney?" Dr. Cream asks his assistant Lily, telling her the story of "the little boy from Hell's Kitchen, who went out west and made good in Chicago". So McBirney, now on the lam, has to leave his old name and life behind, and change his face, "so that no cop will ever know me", if he wants to be able "walk right up to Chan and say 'Hi ya, Charlie'" before he lets him "have it".

We have *two* famous investigators on hand this time: our favorite detective Charlie Chan, and the renowned forensic specialist and psycho-criminology expert Dr. Otto Von Brom, the latter of whom is particularly proud and protective of his reputation; "...an insult to my ability" and "how dare you insinuate..." the good doctor huffs at any perceived slight or disrespect. Believer of his own hype, and under the assumption that Chan's reputation must be as important to Chan as his own is to him, he wonders aloud if Chan is "afraid to cross wits" with him in a proposed radio debate over the old Rocke case, then insinuates that Chan is leaving town because of the threat issued to him by the still at-large McBirney. Of course, that isn't the case, "but it might look that way if you don't accept his challenge" Jimmy muses, concerned for his father's standing. "Make same in presence of offspring's classmates?" Chan enquires, pretending that such things are of concern to him.

Inspector O'Matthews is right when he says that Chan wouldn't fall for this kind of "phony challenge", but something else about the setup of the radio broadcast - namely host Dr. Cream's anxiousness that Chan should attend - piques Chan's interest, so he plays along and agrees to take part in the debate.

The film opens in a court of law, with Steve McBirney (Marc Lawrence) being found guilty of murder and given the death penalty, based on evidence and testimony provided by Charlie Chan. After being sentenced to be executed on December 9 - "Thanks judge, now I won't have to do any Christmas shopping" he bitterly retorts - McBirney turns to Chan, assuring him that "I won't forget this, while I'm alive". After being escorted from the court room, McBirney grabs the deputy's gun, shooting his way out. We know this because a guard comes staggering into the room, shouting the words "McBirney, grabbed the deputy's gun, shooting his way out".

With all exits out of the city blocked, McBirney hides out at a wax museum of crime (!), which doubles as a plastic surgery where criminals get their faces changed (!!), and triples as a broadcast site for a weekly radio show where unsolved crimes are re-enacted on air (!!!) (Screenwriter John Larkin is at his most quirky and off-beat in this one). "Change this map" McBirney says to Dr. Cream, referring to his own face. McBirney's initial plan, after his face change, was to "walk right up to Chan" and "let him have it", but after weeks of hiding out in the museum recuperating from his operation and listening to the weekly Crime League radio broadcast, he comes up with a more satisfying demise for our favorite detective, deciding instead to set up a trap, rigging up Chan's chair at the broadcast to electrocute him. He strong-arms a reluctant Cream into going along with his plan, and to lure Chan to the museum, gets Cream to do a broadcast on the famous Rocke case, "the one case Chan would go for".

The "Rocke case" is a long off-screen back-story involving a number of characters, some of whom we never really see but only hear about, and various parties have a different stake in the game. Though the museum's kooky night watchman, who talks to the wax figures as he goes about his work, and Chan himself do a good job of concisely summarizing this past history, it's worth reiterating just what exactly went down prior to the opening credits:

- Butcher Dagan and Steve McBirney are partners in illegal activities. Also partners with Joe Rocke in honest enterprises.
- Dagan kills using a poison dart and frames Rocke for the murder. Rocke is found guilty and executed based on evidence of Dr. Von Brom.
- McBirney "pumps thirteen bullets" into who he thinks is Dagan, for having framed Rocke. The body is fished out of Lake Michigan by police three months later, and incorrectly indentified as Dagan.
- Meanwhile, the real Dagan has his face changed by Dr. Cream, and assumes a new identity.

It might seem like a confused jumble, and one you may need a scorecard to keep track of, especially once Dr. Von Brom is killed with a poison dart and it's revealed that the real Dagan is somewhere in the museum; a development that raises the stakes for everyone. It requires characters to withhold testimony that would implicate or exonerate others, for one character to pretend to be insane, and for Chan, but not McBirney, to be aware of the rumor that Cream had once operated on the real Dagan ("Don't double-cross me, Doc", McBirney warns Cream at the beginning of the picture, but it turns out the surgeon long ago already had) in order for it all to hold together.

And yet it *does* hold together, contrivances and all. Characters each have their own motives and fears, and their own stake in the game. Dr. Cream in particular has pressure bearing down on him from several directions, and as he begins to wilt under the weight of it all, it falls to his assistant, and our *femme fatale*, Lily Latimer (played marvelously by Joan Valerie) to do what he won't and try to save their lucrative business, defying McBirney and severing the electric chair wires that were set to fry Chan.

Little touches make the second viewing a pleasure also. Agnew's smile when he hears someone say that Dagan is dead, then his irritation when Cream sheepishly tells his that the subject of that night's broadcast has been changed to the Rocke case: "I have no notes on Rocke", he protests, as if *that* were the reason he's put out (and as if *he* would really need them). At first viewing, it looks innocent enough: We know that Cream was forced by McBirney to change the topic of the broadcast last minute in order to lure in Chan, so naturally he'd be sheepish about slipping the change by Agnew at such notice, and Agnew, as a radio professional, would naturally be put out by this late alteration. But on the second pass, when you know about Agnew and of his and Cream's pre-existing relationship, it suddenly works on a whole other level. Later on, when Chan uncovers Cream's hidden surgery, and deduces that Cream operated on Dagan, Agnew comes blustering in, seemingly demanding Cream to tell Chan who Dagan is.

In truth, CHARLIE CHAN AT THE WAX MUSEUM tends to be overrated. Sure, there's horror trappings and atmosphere to spare. There's shadow and darkness and thunder and rain and lightning and trap doors and sliding panels and hidden rooms and wax figures and mummy bandages, and it's all wrapped up and lovingly packaged with spooky lighting and titled camera angles, but it's all superficial and cosmetic. Under the skin, there's not a whole lot at its core, and the film is neither consistently engaging nor particularly gripping. Its all sizzle and no steak, all icing and no cake. Very tasty, but not entirely filling or satisfying.

The beginning of World War II in Europe saw the loss of that market for the Chan series, and a reduction in the size and scope of the films resulted. Following the big adventure caper CHARLIE CHAN IN PANAMA, and the vast, expansive sea voyage that was CHARLIE CHAN'S MURDER CRUISE, CHARLIE CHAN AT THE WAX MUSEUM, for the most part confined to the one set (albeit a big, rich and elaborately decorated one, complete with a chamber of horrors and an electric chair), is a considerably more constrained and claustrophobic affair. We're also down, from MURDER CRUISE's 77 minutes, to a 63 minute runtime. From the upper "B" / lower "A" status enjoyed by Chan films past, we're heading firmly toward "B" Movie territory now. But while this film about reputations may not be quite as good as its own, there are still plenty of thrills, surprises, and delights.

Pass the popcorn.

BEST MOMENT: [30:51] - The murder of Dr. Von Brom. "It is imperative to broadcast this night", Dr. Von Brom insists, having realized the mistake he previously made in the Rocke case, and having now worked out the truth. "To the radio I will tell the police where to find the real murderer" he proclaims. The party sit down at the table to begin the broadcast, Dr. Cream directing Chan to the seat that he and McBirney have booby-trapped for him, "I sit there" says Von Brom, wanting to replicate the setting of the original murder exactly, but Dr. Cream sternly insists that the seat at the head of the table is for Mr. Chan. The broadcast begins, with Chan sitting in the wired seat, the switch set to be pulled and Chan set to be electrocuted at 8:20, just as McBirney has planned. But just before the fatal moment, the restless Von Brom again insists that the seat at the head of the table should be his, and he and Chan switch seats. Watching in the shadows McBirney and his bodyguard Grenock run to stop the night watchman from pulling the switch, but their too late. 8:20 hits, the switch is pulled, the lights go out, and a large spark lights up behind Von Brom. When the lights return, the doctor, rises from his chair, and slumps forward onto the table. He's dead.

But it wasn't the electrocution that killed him. "Wire to chair previously severed by wire cutters. Dr. Von Brom *not* electrocuted", Chan notes. The Criminologist "was murdered", hit by a poison dart shot when the lights went out. We learn that Dr. Cream's assistant Lily cut the cable, to foil McBirney's plan and save her and Cream's business. But in preventing one murder, she inadvertently created the perfect opportunity for another, enabling Von Brom's killer to strike in the cover of the darkness. Great writing!

IN SHORT: Gloriously gimmicky entry with props galore and horror trappings to spare. Good "rainy Saturday afternoon in" fun.

MURDER OVER NEW YORK (1940)

"Coincidence like ancient egg - leave unpleasant odor"
- Charlie Chan

Sidney Toler (Charlie Chan), **Sen Yung** (Number Two Son Jimmy) **Marjorie Weaver** (Patricia West), **Robert Lowery** (David Elliott), **Ricardo Cortez** (George Kirby), **Donald MacBride** (Inspector Vance), **Melville Cooper** (Herbert Fenton), **Joan Valerie** (June Preston), **Kane Richmond** (Ralph Percy), **John Sutton** (Richard Jeffery), **Leyland Hodgson** (Boggs), **Clarence Muse** (Butler), **Frederick Worlock** (Hugh Drake), **Lal Chand Mehra** (Ramullah).

Director: **Harry Lachman**
Screenplay: **Lester Ziffren**
Runtime: 65 mins. 20th Century-Fox Film Corp.

Film 24 in the Charlie Chan *series.*

SYNOPSIS: Charlie Chan takes over the hunt for an elusive saboteur when the Investigator originally on the case is murdered.

Son (II)

Immediately apparent upon examination of MURDER IN NEW YORK is the fact that it is the first Charlie Chan film since THE BLACK CAMEL some 22 pictures earlier not to have our favorite detective's name in its title. Officially there was nothing sinister here, at the time it was still promoted very much as a Charlie Chan film, this unfamiliar labeling simply an attempt to distinguish it from the others, lest potential audiences mistook this new, first run Chan from an old one.

Though one could hardly have blamed them if they had. First of all, virtually the whole cast of MURDER IN NEW YORK had starred in previous Chan films. Not including Sidney Toler and Sen Yung, six of the seven names in cast title card at the beginning of the film will be familiar to Chan fans:

We have Marjorie Weaver (who played Paula Drake in CHARLIE CHAN'S MURDER CRUSIE), Robert Lowery (who was also in MURDER CRUSIE as Dick Kenyon, played Wally Burke in CHARLIE CHAN IN RENO, and had a brief bit as one of the reporters in CHARLIE CHAN ON BROADWAY), Ricardo Cortez (Dr. Ainsley in RENO), Donald MacBride (who played another law enforcement man, Police Chief Kilvaine in CHARLIE CHAN AT TREASURE ISLAND), Joan Valerie (memorable as *femme fatale* Lilly Latimer in CHARLIE CHAN AT THE WAX MUESUM), Kane Richmond (Curtis Whitman in RENO), and, not credited, Frank Coughlin Jr. (who played the jockey Eddie Brill in CHARLIE CHAN AT THE RACE TRACK and has another bit role here as a hat check boy).

Drawn once more from the rich well of reliable 20th Century-Fox contract players, all are back, most in similar type roles. Were we not missing perhaps the most distinctive three, the stern, suave Douglas Dumbrille, future THE BLOB (1958) screen-writer Kay Linaker, and Marc Lawrence as a gangster, we've have the full roster of perennial Chan players all present and accounted for. These familiar faces are always welcome, but rarely have the usual suspects been so usual.

Next, the location and the plot. Chan finds himself back in New York (as he was in CHARLIE CHAN ON BROADWAY), taking over a case after the death of a Scotland Yard Investigator and "old friend" (a familiar plot point seen in CHARLIE CHAN'S MURDER CRUISE, among others), in a story that sees the war angle is again played up with a plot involving sabotage (see also CHARLIE CHAN IN PANAMA), this time of US-built bomber planes bound for Brittan.

Following the eccentric, intricate and idiosyncratic CHARLIE CHAN AT THE WAX MUSEUM, MURDER OVER NEW YORK takes a straight forward, back-to-basics approach, in keeping with a war time piece. Solid and up to the mark, if not overly colorful, it sticks to the point, its focus firmly on the story and on the mystery, and from this angle it succeeds in keeping one interested intrigued.

On board a plane bound for New York, Chan has a chance meeting with Hugh Drake, an old friend and former Scotland Yard Investigator who has moved over to Military Intelligence for the war effort. Drake explains that he's currently trailing the wife of master saboteur Paul Narvo. He takes up Chan's offer for assistance, Chan remarking that "British tenacity and Chinese patience like royal flush in poker game: Unbeatable". Their conversion suggests that a collaboration between the two detectives is in the works, a nice bit of misdirection that aids in making it at least somewhat surprising when the inevitable happens a scene or two later. As they touch down in New York, Chan and Drake make plans to meet up later that evening.

Later that evening, Chan and Jimmy arrive at the apartment of George Kirby, who is hosting a party for Drake. They enter the study where Drake is working, to find Drake slumped over the desk, dead. Chan notices that the caged canary nearby is also dead, attributing the death of both man and bird to a gas pellet they find on the floor - "canary, unlike faithful dog, do not die for sympathy". Jimmy identifies the gas as tetragene, a new gas that "kills with one whiff then evaporates leaving a slight harmless scent". They also discover that Drake's briefcase, which contained Paul Narvo's photo and fingerprints, is missing.

Establishing that it must have been an inside job, names and fingerprints of guests and servants - the only ones in the apartment - are collected. Here our suspects, the guests of the party, are all clearly introduced, their relationships or otherwise with the victim neatly established - Some specifically invited because the late Drake, presumably in his hunt for Narvo, wanted to meet them, others arranging an invitation because *they* wanted to meet *him*. But then, Jimmy catches the butler Boggs in the kitchen steaming open a cablegram, the contents of which allude to his possible guilt. Though Boggs protests his innocence, insisting he has been falsely accused, he is handcuffed and taken away. With the butler in custody, the guests are permitted to leave. Though they're asked to write down their addresses and contact details as they do so, and told not to leave the city, it seems that this is a "cut and dried case".

But just when it seems that Chan and Jimmy have this nut cracked, it's revealed that there was another person, not part of the party, who visited Drake in the study that evening...

We then cut to this other person, David Elliott, who as it happens, is an expert in chemical research. With him is Patricia West, the wife of the saboteur Drake was pursing: Narvo. Patricia long ago fled from her husband upon discovering his activities, and has been hopping around the world avoiding him, and Drake, ever since. She knows nothing of the whereabouts of Narvo, but fears that Drake will never let up on her. David says he loves her and won't let her run away again, which is why he went to see Drake that evening to talk to him. They seem to have no idea that Drake has been killed, but here we have the wife of Narvo, and an expert in the same lethal gas that Narvo's pursuer was killed with, together, and though innocent they may be ("you're innocent. We'll prove it" David insists), it doesn't look good for this fledging couple.

Perhaps this is all simply a symptom of the series becoming increasingly formulaic, but this straightforward storytelling serves the movie well. The story flows well from one scene to next, following a well structured daisy chain of events, from Patricia's apartment where Jimmy tangles with Narvo's aide Ramullah, to the police headquarters where Ramullah is identified but then killed, to Ramullah's East Indian curio-shop where the deadly gas was manufactured, etc. And there are plenty of interesting clues to help Chan and Jimmy make each next step, including a dead canary, a missing pearl, a briefcase containing a set of the saboteur's fingerprints, and a police line-up consisting of every Hindu in New York, including Shemp Howard!

But while the approach may be no-frills, it's not entirely no-thrills, saving itself for its gripping finale with Chan and suspects on aboard a bomber plane for its test flight over New York City, with canister of poison gas that teeters precariously on a ledge inside, and only the one person there who knows the sabotage plot can keep from breaking, simultaneously saving and exposing himself. It's a figuratively and literally heightened version of the trap Chan set in CHARLIE CHAN IN PANAMA (though unlike IN PANAMA, this one requires an additional scene afterwards to expose the real killer and tie up the lose ends).

It's in this film as much as any other that we see the real difference between the Toler/Yung dynamic, and that of the old Oland/Luke pairing. Number Two Son's surprise greeting for his father at the airport is a similar set up to Number One Son's arrival at the docks in CHARLIE CHAN IN SHANGHAI, but it doesn't garner quite the same response from Pop, with neither the "joy" nor the "astonishment" that the earlier Chan had for the earlier son's entrance evident here. This is in keeping with Toler's different interpretation of the role, but, aside from being now played more for comedy, also shows the two sons as different characters and at different stages of their life. Lee was older, more his own man, with his own job and own life, while the younger Jimmy here is "playing hooky" from the "expensive education" Chan is paying for. Both sons are devoted to their Pop and committed to helping him on his cases, but Lee was more obedient, more reverential and respectful, as befitting a first born, but also more vociferous, while Jimmy, although shyer, is more imposing of himself in a different way, perhaps with more to prove, but becoming more cock-sure now that he *can* prove it, and more convinced of what a difference to solving the case his presence will make.

In return, Toler's Chan is a little more sarcastic toward his Number Two Son, knocking him with deflating - but amusing and not too cruel - remarks whenever he gets too brash or forgets himself. When Jimmy arrives at the airport, Chan introduces him to Inspector Vance with "This is favorite offspring, Jimmy, without whose assistance, many cases would have been solved much sooner", to which Jimmy frowns and casts his eyes downward sheepishly. But if Jimmy is deterred by being the butt of the joke, it's only ever momentarily, his enthusiasm and confidence always quickly rejuvenated and renewed. Even Chan's other quips, such as "Number Two Son very promising detective - promise very much, produce very little", and "will inform honorable mother that aid from number two son like interest on mortgage - impossible to escape" can dent Jimmy's confidence only for a second.

At the wash-up, Jimmy, for whom success wipes clean all memory of any ordeals or problems encountered in obtaining same, rather boastfully declares the case to have been easy, to which Chan, in what is perhaps the most astute summation of his Number Two Son ever, observes that "Confidence of favorite son like courage of small boy at dentist: Most evident after tooth extracted." But the funniest moment comes much earlier, when Chan and Jimmy are making their way to Kirby's to visit Drake. Jimmy is pleased to discover that his father is already working on a case. "Then it's a good thing I came then, isn't it?" he beams, Chan's ensuing silence perhaps the most cutting barb of all.

MURDER OVER NEW YORK isn't the most distinctive or distinguished film in the *Charlie Chan* series, nor is it perhaps the most inventive, sticking to the base formula without building a whole lot new upon it, but the time passes briskly and enjoyably, and there's always something going on, with plenty of interesting bits of business along the way. That the plotting flows well helps (even if the supporting players tend to drift in and out of the story). And its restraint in muting the comedy and forgoing the excess, committing instead to a more straightforward and focused style, works in its favor. It's less exotic and more practical than most of the other Chans, and aside from a few choice moments it lacks director Harry Lachman's usual stylish flair, but it's good, solid, well made entertainment. That shouldn't be taken as faint praise.

BEST MOMENT: [59:34] - As with CHARLIE CHAN IN PANAMA, the highlight of this film is the finale. A poison-filled gas pellet is placed inside the plane by the saboteur the night before the plane's test flight, the pellet positioned on a ledge in such a way that it will drop and break when the plane goes into its dive, killing the pilots and anyone else aboard.

The next morning Chan requests the presence at the plane's test flight of everyone connected to the case. The guest board the plane, thinking they're doing so only for a tour of the interior while the plane is on the ground, and are shocked when the engines start and the plane takes off with them aboard. "Pop, Pop! Can't you do something?" Jimmy cries, as the plane gathers speed and makes its assent, but Chan just sits there stoically as everyone else hangs on for dear life.

Chan observes the reactions of all around him. Only the one person aboard who knows about the sabotage plot, who knows about the canister of tetragene, can save them all, but in doing so will also expose themselves. Finally, the plane goes into its descent. The canister rolls off the ledge, and on hand to catch it is...

IN SHORT: Enjoyable, straightforward wartime outing, boasting a great climax.

DEAD MEN TELL (1941)

"Man has learned much who has learned how to die"
- Charlie Chan

Sidney Toler (Charlie Chan), **Sen Yung** (Number Two Son Jimmy), **Sheila Ryan** (Kate Ransome), **Robert Weldon** (Steve Daniels), **Don Douglas** (Jed Thomasson), **Katharine Aldridge** (Laura Thursday), **Paul McGrath** (Charles Thursday), **George Reeves** (Bill Lydig), **Truman Bradley** (Captain Kane), **Ethel Griffies** (Miss Nodbury), **Lenita Lane** (Dr. Anne Bonney), **Milton Parsons** (Gene La Farge).

Director: **Harry Lachman**
Screenplay: **John Larkin**
Runtime: 60 mins. 20th Century-Fox Film Corp.

Film 25 in the Charlie Chan *series.*

SYNOPSIS: Charlie Chan searches for a murderer among a party of treasure hunters.

Reason

Like CHARLIE CHAN AT THE WAX MUSEUM, DEAD MEN TELL is a tale whose activity is confined primarily to one very large, richly decorated set... only more so. Like CHARLIE CHAN AT THE WAX MUSEUM, it relies on clever direction, striking cinematography, inventive camera angles and moody lighting to create ambiance and atmosphere, getting the absolute most mileage that can out of its narrow confines and compensating for its claustrophobic setting... only more so. And like CHARLIE CHAN AT THE WAX MUSEUM, it has a highly quirky John Larkin script, brimming with peculiar characters, bizarre ideas, and clever twists... only more so. Both films are highly enjoyable to watch, but while CHARLIE CHAN AT THE WAX MUSEUM runs only skin deep, DEAD MEN TELL has, buried beneath its base premise of murder among fortune seekers, a hidden treasure of thematic riches; motifs of desire, fear, greed, personal growth, superstition, and, for Captain Kane, obsession.

Captain Kane, master of the old-fashioned sailing ship due to set sail for Cocos Island on a $60million treasure hunt cruise in the morning, has a personal rule: "I never meet my passengers until we clear port". He puts his curious article of faith down to an old superstition, but he has his reasons. It's also his reason for wanting "no coppers or coppers kids" aboard the ship when it sails, as he says in response to the news that Jimmy Chan has again been attempting to stowaway on the cruise. And as for his non-negotiable insistence that "we gotta sail in the morning" - his curt response when tour organizer Daniels approaches him with the news that Miss Nodbury, owner of the treasure map, wants to postpone the trip - he has his reasons for that as well. Looking out into the sea, his back turned to society, he stands an isolated and solitary figure; isolated and solitary, one feels, by his own choice. But why?

Miss Patience Nodbury, the one who "cooked up" this treasure hunt in the first place, has her reasons for now wanting to postpone the trip. She's convinced that there's a thief among the party. "Someone broke into my hotel room today, looking for my treasure map" she whispers. But she was too crafty for that, dividing the map into four pieces and secretly distributing the other three segments amongst her fellow passengers.

But the would-be thief is crafty too. Despite the fact that the ship isn't scheduled to depart until the next morning, he's managed to summon each of the party to arrive on board that very night, with hopes of obtaining the four pieces of the map and putting together himself.

And these passengers, an eclectic and eccentric assortment of people if ever there was one, each have their own reasons, beyond the $60 million on offer, for joining the cruise.

The tall, dark, nervous Gene La Farge suffers from a debilitating anxiety neurosis that he's hoping the sea adventure will help alleviate. As his personal physiatrist Dr. Bonney, who is accompanying him, explains, La Farge has a "fear of facing unpleasant situations. His impulse is to always run away from trouble". Jimmy sees nothing wrong with this, but as Chan knows, "trouble like first love, teach many lessons", for "difficulties can only be overcome by facing them", and the peculiar La Farge will never grow beyond his present childlike state unless he can overcome his fear.

Film star Charles Thursday, and his new bride Laura, see the cruise as an opportunity for a perfect private honeymoon. But despite hopes of travelling incognito, he can't escape the trappings of fame, and is soon recognized - then asked for an autograph - mere seconds after having his cover blown. "I can see this trip is going to give us as much privacy as a feature preview" he sighs to his wife.

Journalist Bill Lydig says he's on the job, covering the expedition for his newspaper, while coin expert Jed Thomasson says he's on holiday, having "dreamed for years about life aboard an old sailing ship: Adventure! The South Seas!", and though both instantly give us reasons to doubt their stories, we can tell they each have some other ulterior motive for being on the ship, while Steve Daniels, the organizer, and typist Kate Ransome, who isn't Daniels' girlfriend yet but wish him luck, make up the rest of the party. The members of the cruise are introduced to us incrementally over the first half hour, each arriving at the ship in response to a message they thought was from Daniels (but was actually from the thief) telling them to check out of their respective hotels come on board immediately, and this drawn out structure is a success, giving the story and the characters plenty of room to breathe.

And Chan, on this faithful fog-filled night, has arrived on the *Suva Star* to find his Number Two Son Jimmy, who, in search of adventure, has been attempting to stow away on the cruise; Chan keen to "return young sea hawk to nest of college books" (just as Thursday can't escape his fame, nor, it seems, can Jimmy escape the family business, with his father, and then a murder case, following him not far behind). Toler cuts a stern figure of genuine authority in his long black overcoat and hat as he pokes and prods around the boat, meeting each of the voyagers, then, after the murder is committed, trying to instill order amidst the chaos.

Miss Nodbury is killed, frightened to death by our crafty thief, who exploits her weak heart, and her belief in the legend of the Nodbury family's own grim reaper, Captain Black Hook Nodbury, by guising up as the notorious pirate - complete with iron hook and wooden leg - and re-enacting his fabled ritual (see best moment). As Miss Nodbury hits the floor, leaving this life for the next, he snatches her piece of the map from her dead hand. One down, three to go.

Miss Nodbury's body is discovered, and with her having died of heart failure, there is, unusually for a Chan film, some doubt as to whether she was in fact murdered. But Chan knows a murder when he sees one, and his suspicion is confirmed when the costume used to frighten her, and the piece of the map the killer took from her, are found, having been stashed away on the ship by the killer. "My theory, person who desire secret of treasure map would kill for same. All who have map fragments stand in danger of death" warns Chan, and his appeal manages to net him two more of the pieces, with their owners, Laura and Thomasson, owning up to having been sent them by Miss Nodbury as they had them over. But the fourth piece remains at large, and so too, does the killer.

Absent throughout all this activity, is Captain Kane. "Do you know none of us have ever seen Captain Kane?" Dr. Bonney says to Chan. Later, Chan finally tracks down the elusive Captain. Venturing into the pier's sail loft, Chan finds, buried amid the sails, mast, ropes, nets, chains, and other equipment, Captain Kane, alone at his desk way back at the far end of the room, symbolic of the distance Kane has put between himself and all other people. We learn the motive behind Kane's seemingly unusual behavior, and the meaning behind the words squawked by his talking parrot: "leave you to die as you left me to die", as Chan concludes that the "mystery Captain who avoid passengers have secret reason".

Kane says that Chan is guessing, but Chan's guesses are very good, including his suspicion that Kane knows who the killer is. "We were partners once" he confirms, recounting the story of how they had once searched Cocos Island for Black Hook's treasure years earlier, and had even found markers left by the pirates, albeit ones the two treasure seekers couldn't decipher. But greed took over, and killer left Kane stranded on the island to die, while he left to raise money for a more thorough search. Left for certain death on the deserted island, Kane was saved only by a passing whale ship.

Years later, Kane and the killer now both go by different names, hence why Kane has avoided meeting the passengers, so that his enemy, who is among the party members, won't recognize him. When Miss Nodbury and Daniels publically announced the venture, he knew his enemy would join the cruise. "He jumped at the bait. He's here now".

But Kane has yet to make his move. "Name, please" orders Chan, who wants simply to apprehend the killer, but Kane won't budge. He has other plans. "I'm going to leave him on the island to starve, the way he left me" he says.

"He left me marooned without water in the boiling sun" Kane remembers. But while others may have been grateful to have survived the ordeal, to have escaped death and to still be alive, Kane has become consumed by obsession, driven only by his thoughts of revenge, of hearing his "hated one" cry out the words "Help! Help! Let me out of here". Scarred, blackened by his experience, he's turned his back on society and on all people, and as he sits there, smoking his pipe, with only his parrot to talk to, one wonders if Kane ever really escaped, or if he's still there, marooned on the island.

Even his desk, a sea of maps and charts and papers obtained from the killer's luggage, is a monument to his obsession. "It's proof. Proof of what he's planning" he rages. Should Kane get to the killer before Chan, we know that this extremely driven man will overpower his target.

And so he does at the end, as he seizes on his nemesis, overpowering his hated adversary and getting him on his knees. Interestingly, there's no moment of recognition on behalf of the former partner, who you might think would have been wide-eyed shocked to see a man he left for dead years ago suddenly staring him right in the face (that he isn't just goes to show that obsession really is a one way street), but *Kane* remembers, and now he finally has what he has so fervently craved since that day when he was stranded on the island. You can see in his eyes and hear in his voice that he has been waiting for the moment, and you know that he will do to his former partner all that he has previously claimed he would. But before he can, Chan steps in, announcing that the law will take care of the killer. "I suppose that will have to do" Kane grumbles as he hands his captive - now fated to go not to the island to die, but instead to prison - over to Chan, but one wonders if it really will.

All the characters of DEAD MEN TELL board the ship in search for something - whether it be material riches or some sort of personal fulfillment or satisfaction - but no one comes away what it was they were seeking. The killer doesn't get his treasure, and Kane doesn't get his revenge. Miss Nodbury dies, but doesn't get to meet her Grandfather. The Thursdays don't get their private honeymoon, and while Daniels expresses a romantic interest in Kate, there's nothing to suggest either way that anything will develop. The four pieces of the map are obtained, but they are never put together. And Jimmy, while falling into the water no less than for times, doesn't get his sea adventure, his attempts to stow away on the ship thwarted first by Kane, then by Chan, then by the cancelation of the voyage.

But the neurotic, phobic La Farge, who earlier in the film ran from Miss Nodbury's dead body, then failed in his chance to speak up about it, seems, by the end, to have made at least the first tentative steps toward some sort of cure. "I've always wanted to do that to someone" is his stark explanation for leading Jimmy off the plank and into the water, suggesting that he's learning audacity, if not impulse control. But that he doesn't, despite asking for it, get back his piece of the map at the end suggests that he still has some way to go.

DEAD MEN TELL is as remarkable for what there isn't and for what there is, with a captain who never meets his passengers, on a ship that never leaves, for a treasure hunt that never happens, because of a back-story we never get to see. All for a divided treasure map that's never completely put together belonging to a legendary pirate who never shows up to fulfill his prophecy.

This anchored setting was bound to give the action a circular feel, and at times it does, as the characters poke and prod around their detailed but narrow confines - from the cold, fog-laden docks, to the noisy, rambunctious bar filled with drunks and bottom dwellers, and in and out and around and around the cabins and hulls and nooks and crannies of the majestic wooden ship itself. Several characters are at various points dispatched to find a telephone and call the police, but whether or not they make it is something we can't always determine. If we could see through the fog we might be able see what, if anything, exists beyond the sets perimeters, the fixed lanterns scattered around the shipyard not so much piecing though the thick soup of fog as shining dimly behind it, as the set's inhabitants wander around a universe that won't let them leave. "How does one get out of this shipyard?" La Farge asks at one point, as if such a thing were possible. Later, when the case is seemingly over and the party are finally permitted to leave the ship, they disappear off-screen, last heard searching for an exit: "Where can we get a taxi?" "At the corner. If we can find the corner"...

All this from a film whose title card - of the eagerly sort after treasure map in one piece - and opening shot - of a sign bragging of a $60,000,000 bounty - suggested an epic adventure. "I didn't know there was that much dough in the whole world" a lady exclaims during the opening shot as she passes the sign. "There ain't!" says her weary companion, seizing her by the arm and dragging her away before she can get any bright ideas about joining the expedition, as if he knows that the boat ain't going nowhere. And on first viewing, if you were expecting the treasure hunt, then you too may feel, once it becomes apparent that the cruise has been called off and ship isn't going to sail, that this film is one that never leaves the starting gate. But once you realize that the ship isn't going anywhere and neither is anyone else, and once you adjust yourself to the rather claustrophobic setting, you'll see that you're in for something rather special.

If not always to be taken literally. The pirate costume was designed to work only the superstitious and susceptible Miss Nodbury, so why should the killer think to don it again at the end (particularly the cumbersome wooden leg)? But just because something doesn't make literal sense, doesn't mean it doesn't make sense *thematically*. This film has its own internal logic; the sound of the peg leg hitting the boardwalk at the finale lets everyone know that the killer is approaching. Look at the close up of Jimmy as he turns his head upon hearing the ominous tapping (and of course, the killer *has* to wear the pirate mask, so that Chan can unmask him).

Because DEAD MEN TELL is art, and art doesn't always have to be literal. If the Chan pictures were by this point contracting rather than expanding in terms of size and scope, they at least weren't going down without a fight, as this little miracle of mood, atmosphere and suspense testifies.

There are so many, many beautiful composed frames, each of them positively exquisite and each of them containing something special; the interiors of the ship (apparently Kane had been using it as a museum until now) positively loaded with props (such the 'Iron Maiden' spiked torture chamber). And instead of a music score, the film utilizes the surrounding sounds of the shipyard, with foghorns and ships bells, the gentle rocking of the water, and the haunting melody of an ocarina, carrying through the air over the stark silence. Like the film as a whole, it's a daring choice, and like the film as a whole, it really works.

BEST MOMENT: [7:14] - Searching for Jimmy on board the ship, Chan meets Miss Nodbury, owner of the treasure map and organizer of the pending expedition. Their conversation turns to the ship's museum pieces, including the portraits on the wall of famous pirates, Chan noting that one of them, Black Hook Nodbury, shares the same last name as his interlocutor.

"My grandfather" she nods, "he made the map I found". She turns to her grandfather's picture and directly addresses it: "You needn't come for me tonight, Black Hook. I'm not ready".

"Come for you?" Chan asks, seemingly on the fence in regards to the old lady's sanity. She explains to Chan the legend of her pirate ancestor: "He was hanged for murder and piracy, over 100 years ago. And every time a Nodbury dies, he comes to escort us into the other world. First, you hear the tap of his wooden leg, then the scratch of his iron hook on the door", then adds "we Nodburys are not afraid".

Chan is suitably impressed. "Man has learned much who has learned how to die".

IN SHORT: Director Lachman and writer Larkin are at their most inventive in this atmospheric little piece. Thematically rich, with something special in nearly every frame.

CHARLIE CHAN IN RIO (1941)

"Interesting problem in Chemistry: sweet wine often turn nice woman sour"
- Charlie Chan

Sidney Toler (Charlie Chan), **Sen Yung** (Number Two Son Jimmy), **Mary Beth Hughes** (Joan Reynolds), **Cobina Wright, Jr.** (Grace Ellis), **Ted North** (Clark Denton), **Victor Jory** (Alfredo Marana), **Harold Huber** (Chief Souto), **Richard Derr** (Ken Reynolds), **Jacqueline Dalya** (Lola Dean), **Kay Linaker** (Helen Ashby), **Truman Bradley** (Paul Wagner), **Hamilton Mac Fadden** (Bill Kellogg), **Leslie Denison** (Rice), **Iris Wong** (Lili), **Eugene Borden** (Armando), **Ann Codee** (Margo).

Director: **Harry Lachman**
Screenplay: **Samuel G. Engel** and **Lester Ziffren**
Runtime: 61 mins. 20th Century-Fox Film Corp.

Film 26 in the Charlie Chan *series. A remake of THE BLACK CAMEL (1931).*

SYNOPSIS: Charlie Chan arrives in Rio to arrest a murderess and bring her back home to Hawaii to face trial, but before he can apprehend her she herself is murdered.

Love

WARNING: This review reveals the murderer.

The love story element of the Charlie Chan mysteries had been a key part of the formula since the wandering John Quincy Winterslip chanced upon Carlotta Egan in Earl Derr Biggers' very first Chan story, *The House without a Key*, the "innocent couple caught up in the mystery" device being a standard convention of detective fiction of the 1920s and 30s. As the film series progressed beyond the original novels, this romance element, usually of young lovers somehow entangled in the crisis, went from an important and well integrated component of the overall mystery plot (CHARLIE CHAN IN LONDON, CHARLIE CHAN IN PARIS), to diverting, to perfunctory, to obligatory, then to near non-existent (a very slight D-Plot in stories like CHARLIE CHAN AT THE WAX MUSEUM and DEAD MEN TELL), before returning in a big way when the filmmakers returned to Biggers material for Twentieth Century-Fox's 26th and penultimate *Charlie Chan* film, CHARLIE CHAN IN RIO.

CHARLIE CHAN IN RIO, the second filming of *The Black Camel* (following the 1931 Warner Oland Chan film of that name), is a story of love. Of romantic love, obsessive love, tender love and sad love. Of brotherly love, of young love, and of unrequited love. Of the jealousy it can fuel, the hate that it can bring, and the lengths that people will go to because of it. Everyone's motive in CHARLIE CHAN IN RIO, everything that they do, is based on love.

We have Lola Dean, the victim of this piece - though not an innocent one - who when living in Honolulu a year and a half ago under her real name Lola Wagner, "was madly in love" with married man Manuel Cardosa. When Manuel refused to divorce his wife and marry her, Lola killed him. If she couldn't have him, no one would. She then fled Honolulu, winding up in Rio. And now, a year and a half later, Chan and Jimmy, with the help of Rio Chief of Police Souto, have managed to track Lola down, arriving in Rio to arrest her and bring her back to Honolulu to face trial. "She doesn't look like a murderess" Jimmy muses, as they sit in the audience at the club during her nightclub performance, to which Chan responds that "pretty woman, like lapdog, sometimes go mad".

We also have Helen Ashby, the murderess of this piece (or should that be the *second* murderess, after Lola?), who has spend a year, *a year*, in Rio as Lola Dean's secretary, and who, unbeknown to Lola, is really Barbara Cardosa, the widow of the man Lola murdered. Never hinting at what she suspects about her boss, but all the while waiting for her chance, she has "thought of nothing, lived for nothing" than to find the person who killed her husband.

Then there is Alfredo Marana, Helen's collaborator, a renowned psychic who Helen arranges for Lola to have a session with. Alfredo Marana is really Alfredo Cardosa, brother of the man Lola murdered, and brother-in-law of Helen, and the two of them have hatched a plan. In his "psycognosis" session with Lola, Marana provides her with an herbal cigarette that, when consumed and then stimulated by the caffeine of a small cup of coffee, places her a trance-like semi-comatose state, relieving her of her inhibitions and compelling her to tell the truth to questioned asked of her. Clearly anticipating her visit, we hear Marana playing a record of Lola's latest song when she arrives. Now with his subject in this semi-comatose state, he makes a recording of his own, asking her questions over her true identity and how she came to be in Rio, and recording her confession of the murder. He then awakes her from the trance, and though she doesn't remember anything that she has said, he assures her, "considering what you've just revealed...", that her dark secret is a secret no more. He also assures her that he will keep what she revealed to him confidential, but tells her come back to see him again next day "and we'll have a talk".

Helen and Marana intend to hand the confession over to the police the next morning, but Lola doesn't plan to wait around that long. Rightfully afraid that her secret is about to come out, she plans to run, and persuades her new fiancé Clark that they should fly away to the 'States and elope that night. When Lola, readying her luggage, tells Helen the "good news", that she and Clark are running off to elope, Helen releases that she's fleeing again and won't be back, and that she and Marana may never catch her again. "The thought of Lola and Clark living in happiness" too much for her to bear, she kills her.

What makes Helen and Alfredo's fate all the more tragic is that their actions proved unnecessary. Unbeknown to them, Chan was about to arrest Lola anyway. Lola's past *had* caught up with her and justice *was* about to be served. Had they not put their plan for getting a confession out of her in to motion, or even if they'd made Lola's appointment with Marana one day later, Chan would have been able to arrest Lola alive (or, say if Chan had decided to arrest her there at the club, instead of electing to wait until later in the evening so as to avoid causing a scandal). Helen and Alfredo would have seen justice done, but at no cost to their freedom. Or their lives. Or their souls.

Think of this all from the murderesses point of view. Your husband is murdered, but his death is written off as a suicide and the woman who killed him gets away. You and your brother-in-law follow the clues yourself and manage to track her down. You spend a year as her secretary - a year spending every day standing next to the woman you suspect murdered your husband - smiling at her, taking her orders. Finally, you're able to put your plan into motion and you get a confession out of her, and you can now take to the police proof of what she has done. But then she gets engaged and gives you the news that she's going away, and though she doesn't explicitly say forever, you know that she means forever. Suddenly, it looks like she's about to flee again, and jet off into the sunset with her new fiancé for a happy ending. You can't bear the idea of her living in happiness, of her escaping retribution again, so you kill her, only to get a knock on the door moments later, and find out that the police were about to arrest her anyway! That it's Helen, and not Lola, being handcuffed and hauled away for murder at the end is a tragedy, one as much of circumstance and happenstance as anything else. "Fruits of labor sometimes very bitter" Chan notes upon being congratulated for uncovering this not completely unsympathetic killer, one who has somehow become the very thing she hated: someone who killed out of love. And there's a moment where Marana, in one last desperate act of love, tries honorably to take the fall for his late brother's widow, but Chan sees through it. And anyway, Helen won't hear of it. "I can't pretend any longer" she says, proving that she's at least not completely as corrupt as Lola.

From the beginning of the film, where the jealously positively drips from the tongues of Grace Ellis and Joan Reynolds - two women who both covet men who in turn covet Lola, with one happier than the other to hear that Clark is taking the singer off the market - we see how the sweet wine of love can leave a sour aftertaste. And Lola, it turns out, also had an ex-husband of her own, Paul Wagner, who, still very much carrying a torch for his ex-wife, has arrived in Rio to try and win her back. "It must be heavenly to be in love", sighs Lily, Lola's housemaid, after hearing of Lola and Clark's engagement. Well, maybe not always.

The screenwriters and director have used the original *The Black Camel* story to craft a solid murder mystery. Chan fans and mystery buffs should enjoy it. Though it's somewhat dramatically lacking in places, there is little comedy relief, and it's all played straight and taken seriously.

Sidney Toler and Harold Huber (as the local Chief of Police, in his most subdued and agreeable Chan appearance) are effective in their roles as driving protagonists, leading the viewer through the procedural investigation like a pair of old pros, dismantling the fake clues and theorizing over the real ones. Their easygoing but focused conjecturing befits experienced professionals. It's just a pleasure to watch. Following their "long shot", they search for scratch marks left on the floor from a pin that was embedded in the shoe of the killer when she stepped on Lola's broach from Clark.

If there's a flaw in the drama, it's that we never really get to see what Clark, Lola's fiancé, makes of it all. Yes, he's shown to be in shock, and other characters are appropriately sympathetic (someone mentions taking a vacation in Maine, "when this is all over"), but his reaction to hearing the news of Lola's death, and then to the startling revelations of her past and her recorded confession is played for all to here, is never really captured.

One also questions the second murder, of the butler Rice who saw what Helen had done, and who she tried to buy off with Lola's jewels. It seems out of character for the murderess, who, at this point would have accepted, as she does a few minutes later, that the game was up (it might have made more sense for Marana, trying to protect his sister-in-law, to have shot Rice, but this would have required an opportunity for Helen to get him alone to tell him of Rice's discovery). But these are just minor quibbles.

CHARLIE CHAN IN RIO was the only of the final four Twentieth Century-Fox Chan films to have our favorite detective's name in the title. It's also the only of the final four that sees the series attempting to advance rather than retreat, in its efforts, like a number Hollywood films of early 40's, to capture a South American market (to replace the European one lost due to the war). It's not the most polished of the Chan films, as evident in the scene where the drunken Joan is so inebriated she believes she's in Honolulu simply because she heard someone say the word "Honolulu" (the "coffee and cigarettes" device also perhaps works a little too well), but it's slick and it's glossy and it's hugely entertaining from beginning to end. From the dramas and the jealousy between "friends" who don't particularly like each other, to Bill Kellogg's nerdy interest in the case, to Jimmy's humorous confessions while under hypnosis, there are number of amusing interactions between characters, a change from the broader comedy more common in the series. There's also lively opening samba dance in the nightclub, followed by Lola's amorous "Midnight Serenade" number.

Throughout the film, there's a cute runner concerning Jimmy fledgling romance with Lily, the house maid, a sweet courtship that culminates with them dancing under the moonlight. Just prior to that, there's a lovely scene of the two of them standing by a fish bowl. He coyly advances. Then, when she suggestively pushes back, he shyly recoils, only to come forward again. Love is a running theme through this film, and in a story where nearly every other character has a tragic tale of love to tell, of a love that has either ended or is coming to end, we have in Jimmy and Lily a potential love story just blossoming, and by the end of the film, Jimmy states his intentions to take Lily back home to Hawaii with him and marry her. But just as it seems that love will conquer all and that there will be happily ever after for at least this one couple, Jimmy gets the news that he has been drafted to the United States Army.

BEST MOMENT: [40:46] - Marana plays for everyone the record of Lola's confession, but Chan has a revelation of his own: that Marana is really Alfredo Cardosa, brother of the man Lola killed. Stunned, Marana asks how Chan could possibly know this, to which Chan replies "Professional ability: detective".

What Chan *doesn't* know is how Marana was able to get Lola to talk. Marana explains his process of using cigarettes laced with a special herb that, when stimulated by caffeine, put the patient in a semi-comatose state, relieving them of their conscious inhibitions and compelling them to speak the truth.

Chan seems satisfied, but Jimmy is less than impressed, dismissing it as "a lot of phooey". "I might believe it" he says "if not for the semi-comatose stuff". Adamant it won't work, Jimmy agrees to undergo the process himself, and, with Chan's permission, Marana gives Jimmy some coffee and one of his cigarettes. Within seconds the cigarette takes affect, and Marana hands Jimmy over to Chan.

Chan takes this opportunity to question Jimmy. First he asks about recent damage done to the family car. Previously, Jimmy had denied borrowing the car that day, but now, under the hypnosis, he admits that he banged the car into a fire hydrant and was lying earlier. Then, Chan seeks an explanation for his failing grades in his Mathematics course at college. Jimmy reveals that the class starts at 8 in the morning and he too lazy to get up on time. Finally, he demands to know what Jimmy's main interest in the current case is, to which he answers Lily. "She sure is cute. I'd go for her like flies for honey".

Having heard enough, Chan shakes Jimmy from his trance, then wags his finger at him and with rapid fire precision berates his Number Two Son over the items of information he has obtained. "After this you no longer use parents' car, then you not bump into fireplug. Also, you rise very early in the morning in order to attend mathematics class. And keep mind on present investigation and not on pretty Chinese cousin".

Jimmy, stunned and a tad embarrassed, apologizes to Marana for having doubted him. As the others leave the room, Jimmy quietly approaches him. "Uh, is it possible to get...", "Another cigarette, why certainly" Marana finishes, holding out his cigarette case. "For the young lady?" he smiles knowingly.

Jimmy wonders how he guessed, to which Marana reminds him: "Professional ability: mind reader".

IN SHORT: Glossy remake of THE BLACK CAMEL is sloppy in spots, but overall great entertainment.

CASTLE IN THE DESERT (1942)

"Elaborate excuse seldom true"
- Charlie Chan

Sidney Toler (Charlie Chan), **Sen Yung** (Number Two Son Jimmy), **Arleen Whelan** (Brenda Hartford), **Richard Derr** (Carl Detheridge), **Douglas Dumbrille** (Manderley), **Henry Daniell** (Watson King), **Edmund MacDonald** (Walter Hartford), **Lenita Lane** (Lucy Manderley), **Ethel Griffies** (Madame Saturnia), **Milton Parsons** (Fletcher), **Steve Geray** (Dr. Retling), **Lucien Littlefield** (Gleason).

Director: **Harry Lachman**
Screenplay: **John Larkin**
Runtime: 72 mins. 20th Century-Fox Film Corp.

Film 27 in the Charlie Chan *series, and the final from Twentieth Century-Fox.*

SYNOPSIS: Charlie Chan is summoned to the secluded desert castle of an eccentric millionaire to investigate a murder that has yet to actually be committed.

Murder

Inspector Duff, Shelah Faye, Sir Lionel Grey, Dan Winterslip, P.J. Madden, Captain Hamilton, Mademoiselle Nardi, Professor Arnold, Sir Stanley Woodland, Allen Colby, Joe Kinney, Gordon Kent, Enrico Barelli, Test Pilot Edwards, Billie Bronson, Al Rogers, Elise Hillman, Jeanne Bently, Paul Essex, B. Petroff, R.J. Godley, Gerald Pendleton, Dr. Otto von Brom, Inspector Vance, Patience Nodbury, Lola Dean.

These are among the murder victims of the first twenty-six films of the *Charlie Chan* series. Who will be the next to join this ill-fated list? The answer is a little longer in coming than you might think...

Dear Mr. Chan,
   Your presence is most urgently requested at
Manderley Castle for assistance and advice. My
life is in danger.
   Do not communicate with me. A car will await
you each day at noon at Mojave Wells, California.
This note bearing my crest will identify you to my
chauffer. Bring no one else.

   signed
   Mrs. Paul Manderley
   (formerly Princess Lucrezia della Borgia)

So reads the mysterious note slipped under Charlie Chan's hotel room door he and his Number Two Son Jimmy - who is on one-week leave from the Army "for good behavior" - pack for a holiday road trip. Chan has heard before of this strange, secluded castle in the desert owned by the scholarly millionaire Paul Manderley; "no electricity, no telephone" he muses. While Jimmy has heard of the Borgias; "*poisoners*" he shivers. "She's crazy. You can't go there alone" Jimmy exclaims in regard to Mrs. Manderley's insistence that his Pop 'bring no one else', but Chan decides to answer the call and make the journal, and to adhere to the note's peculiar instructions. He also borrows one of Jimmy's signal corps carrier pigeons to take with him, just in case he should need to send for assistance.

We arrive at Manderley Castle a little earlier than Chan, following a Professor Gleeson as his car makes the journey down the harsh, barren desert road, past the guarded iron gates that bear an intimidating "PRIVATE: NO VISITORS" sign, and through the near jungle of uninviting cacti up to the foreboding front door of this famed medieval castle.

Inside, Mrs. Manderley, Lucy, extends to Professor Gleeson a warm welcome that defies the castle's inaccessibility. "Very nice of you to come" she says offering her hand, as he joins the others guests in the sitting room. He remarks that he's heard a great deal about her. "Nice things I hope" she says smilingly, as she goes about mixing cocktails. She begins introducing Gleeson to her other guests, until one of them reminds her it was in fact *them* who invited him. "Where are my wits today" she laughs, realizing her mistake. "I guess I'm not used to having guests" she explains, for "Paul, my husband, prefers to bury himself out here in the desert for work".

But if Mrs. Manderley's warm hospitality refutes the castle's aloof reputation, Mr. Manderley's tetchy hostility reaffirms it. The noise of the group's chatter distracting him from his work, the irritated Manderley stomps into the room to investigate the cause of this damnable ruckus. "Lucy! Who is this stranger?" he asks, indicating Gleeson, "You know I dislike having people interrupt my work". Lucy points out that they do have other guests, Manderley's lawyer Walter Hartford and his wife Brenda, and Manderley's personal physician, Dr. Retling, but Manderley insists that they don't count because they're "here on business".

And Lucy's demeanor too takes a suddenly unsmiling turn upon learning that Gleeson is a genealogist, and when the Professor starts pressing about Lucy's Borgia family heritage, his interest in her ancestry clearly striking a nerve. "Two things we never discuss in this house" she says sternly, "my family and Paul's accident", the second of the twin taboo conversation topics referring to the mask that covers the right side of her husband's face. To lighten the mood, she then jokes that though she is indeed a Borgia, "my branch of the family didn't go for poisoning". Gleeson drops the subject and apologizes, the once again smiling hostess assuring him that "there's nothing to forgive".

Lucy and Mrs. Hartford leave get ready for dinner. Gleeson consumes the cocktail Lucy offered him, and suddenly drops to the floor. He's declared dead by Dr. Retling, who determines that he died of poisoning. Retling and Hartford huddle with Manderley, who, desperate to avoid a scandal, and fearing that his wife will be implicated, convinces the other two men to quietly move the dead man over to the Mojave Wells Hotel, and make it look like he died there of natural causes.

And now it's Chan's turn to pay visit to this castle in the desert. He arrives, carrying with him the small cage containing his commandeered carrier pigeon. "You're responsible for the creature's behavior" the Manderley's valet warns him upon seeing this peculiar item of baggage. Chan tells him not to worry, for the bird is "trained by United States army". To this the unflappable valet doesn't bat an eyelid, suggesting that he's well used to such eccentricities.

Chan takes a look around this strange and eerie castle, examining its tapestries and armor displays, and is soon spotted by Paul Manderley, who was unaware of the detective's arrival, or of his invitation. As unwelcoming and tetchy as ever upon sighting an unsanctioned visitor, his first curt words to Chan are "what are you doing here?" followed by "what do you want?", and then "who are you?"

"Why should my wife send for you?" Manderley wonders aloud after Chan introduces himself. He also seems put out to learn that Chan knows another of his guest, Carl Detheridge, a teacher at Manderley College (another business guest, the only kind of guest that Manderley, it seems, will have), "you two know eachother?" he asks, his accusing eyes darting back and forth between the two of them. Manderley sits Chan down to talk, the scholar believing that Chan has arrived check up on his sanity, because of his "peculiar mode of living". "I'm quite sound, mentally", he insists, though of course no one ever thinks themselves insane. "I'm a historian" he says, explaining that as part of research on the historical Cesare Borgia, about whom he's writing a book, he replicates the 16th Century mode of living, in an attempt to "penetrate the psychology of the 16th century mind" and "understand the workings of the minds of men who lived 400 year ago". "You won't call that insane, would you?" he asks, and indeed he seems quite calm and

183

reasonable, until Chan makes mention of his wife's maiden name of "Borgia". "So what if her name was Borgia?" he demands, as if a switch has just been flicked, "she's just the same as you are, and so am I". Seeing another attack on his sanity forthcoming, he then starts blustering about how he's the executor of a $20 million estate, "an incompetent man couldn't do that?"

As if on queue his personal physician arrives, the agitated Manderley points to him as proof. "Observe me as Dr. Retling does" he challenges Chan, "and prove for yourself whether I'm sane or not". As he storms out of the room, one might say thou doth protest too much, were he not still the sanest seeming person Chan has come across so far to day. But then, he does reside in a world he has created for himself.

Chan then meets Mrs. Manderley, who as she was with Gleeson, is delighted to meet someone new. But though Chan is a welcome guest, it turns out that he's also a surprise one; Lucy revealing that she didn't send for the detective, and that his note, supposedly from her, is a forgery. Writing the matter off as a false alarm, Chan turns to leave when suddenly the valet enters with the shock announcement the car's distributor has been removed. We already know that the castle has "no electricity, no telephone", and with no other transportation on the grounds, and none expected anytime soon - "we may not see a car for weeks" Lucy exclaims - it appears the castle's occupants are stranded. Luckily they have provisions to last for months, and an excellent wine cellar - "I'm happy" Detheridge shrugs, seeing the bright side of their predicament - but stranded they are, nonetheless. "Inhabitants of this castle now marooned 35 miles from civilization" remarks Chan, who also deduces that the note beckoning him to the castle and warning him of impending danger wasn't a false alarm at all, but rather an early one. "Detective sometimes summoned to witness crime" he explains. But no one else will be summoned, it seems, as Chan return to his room to find his carrier pigeon dead. Now with no means of contacting the outside world, they really are isolated. Stranded. Marooned.

CASTLE IN THE DESERT is the story of two isolated people: One, Manderley, who is isolated by his own design, isolated because he wants it that way - "goes around town with half a face. Won't talk civil to nobody" is the Mojave Wells Hotel Manager's scowling description of the standoffish scholar - and the other, Lucy, who is isolated because of circumstance, isolated because of her poisoned family name and because of the irrational fears and prejudices of others. Jimmy makes aspersions of her without having actually met her, "She's crazy", "Borgias. Poisoners" he grimaces, while the people of Mojave Wells deal in rumor and innuendo and hearsay. "She's a queer number", that same Hotel Manager remarks, adamant that "she's put a curse on us".

"My wife and I prefer the solitude of the desert" Manderley continually insists, and although it's clear that *he* is quite content to bury himself in his work and his history books in his rather creepily reconstructed medieval castle, stuck in the past, his head in the sand, completely and utterly incommunicado, one's not as sure about her. For one, she seems positively delighted to meet each and every new guest who arrives at the castle, as if a little starved for human contact, playing the chatty, charming hostess to even complete strangers who arrive uninvited, such as the private detective Fletcher, who, caught trespassing on the grounds, claims to have been hired by Gleeson's family to investigate Gleeson's death. Like Gleeson, Fletcher puts his foot in it by making a remark about Lucy's family history, like Gleeson, he apologies and is seemingly forgiven by the cordial hostess, who invites him to stay for dinner, and like Gleeson, he too then drops dead from poisoning, and again all suspicion turns to the former Borgia Princess.

But the Manderleys aren't the only ones keeping others at arms length. At Mojave Wells, the Hotel Manager, initially welcoming to Chan, cuts him off and banishes him to the stairs upon learning that Chan is waiting for a car from the castle. Then, when the car bearing the crest of the Borgias arrives, Chan thinks he's found a travelling companion for the journey when he meets Watson King, a famous sculptor who is also bound for the castle. But King it seems prefers his own company. "I specialize in minding my own business" he curtly answers when Chan, trying to strike up a conversation, asks about his line of work. "Very lonesome pastime" Chan sighs, as he resigns himself to the fact that travelling to Manderley Castle with Watson King will be akin to travelling alone. But when Chan arrives at the castle and bumps into Detheridge, it's Chan who is the evasive one, at least according to Detheridge, "same old Charlie, he never gives out" he says.

The film actually has dual plots, the first involving the pair of scammers, Retling and Hartford, who it turns out are trying to fleece power of attorney from Manderley (he loses his estate if found incompetent or involved in any notoriety of scandal; the suggestion being that perhaps this clause has made the millionaire a little paranoid and strained, hence his suspicious and isolationist nature). Upon Fletcher's sudden death they try to convince Manderley to have Lucy committed, and to turn control of his estate over to Hartford.

But neither of Lucy's would-be victims are actually dead, Gleeson and Hartford having first Gleeson and then Fletcher to fake being poisoned, in their scheme to con Manderley, and Chan soon uncovers this plot, exonerating Lucy.

The Chan films have always been build around murder, what with them being murder mysteries and all - "what I'd really like is the relaxation of a good murder" says Jimmy, as he rests his weary combat boots at the beginning of the film - but most unusually for a Chan film, we're 50 minutes in and no one, save for one pigeon, has been murdered, and it seems that we might not be in for a murder mystery after all. Could this, the final Twentieth Century-Fox *Charlie Chan* movie, be the first in which there is no murder?

No. Hartford is found in the dudgeon, dead, having been stabbed with an arrow head. The culprit: Lucy's step brother Caesar, who Brenda reveals didn't die in the Spanish War, as everyone believed, but is still alive, having a month earlier written to Hartford for money. And now we have our mystery, and our killer, lurking somewhere within the castle.

The final four Charlie Chan films from Twentieth Century-Fox - MURDER OVER NEW YORK, DEAD MEN TELL, CHARLIE CHAN IN RIO, and CASTLE IN THE DESERT - were all helmed by director Harry Lachman, and all benefit from his stylish eye. Though films were becoming somewhat more formulized in their setup, they were also becoming more distinctively stylish in their execution. All four of these films have their own distinct tones and unique identities. Yet, they can also be grouped into two distinct pairs of type:

1. The first and third, MURDER OVER NEW YORK and CHARLIE CHAN IN RIO, which, both either written or co-written by **Lester Ziffren**, play out as **standard murder mysteries**, and
2. The second and fourth, DEAD MEN TELL and CASTLE IN THE DESERT, which, both scripted by **John Larkin**, play out as **something else entirely**.

MURDER OVER NEW YORK is neat and efficient and linear and compact in its storytelling and construction, Chan and Jimmy' following a neat daisy chain of clues and incidents, one leading to the next as it ascends to its gripping, high altitude finale, while CHARLIE CHAN IN RIO, the last Twentieth Century-Fox Chan film to depict a foreign locale, boasts a slick and glossy sheen, and, is a mystery with the usually trappings played out in the usual way. These two films are more standard and conventional in their intent, MURDER

OVER NEW YORK being a wartime saboteur warning piece, and CHARLIE CHAN IN RIO a murder mystery fuelled by the usual motives of love and revenge. But if this first pair are superior as mystery yarns, then the second two, DEAD MEN TELL and CASTLE IN THE DESERT, are arguably superior as art. For while they both are more quirky, more stylish and more atmospheric than most other Chan films, they both also have more to say on the human condition. How sad it is that the only people the Manderleys can attract are shifty bottom feeders out for their money; the pitfalls of wealth and the perils of cutting yourself off from society interestingly examined.

We know that John Larkin could pen a good Charlie Chan screenplay; he gave us CHARLIE CHAN AT TREASURE ISLAND and DEAD MEN TELL no less. In CASTLE IN THE DESERT we have one high on the contrivances needed to get it up and running, but low on inventive set pieces to keep it going. If the first half is heavy on all the setup that its bizarre premise requires, with the isolated married couple and their remote "no electricity, no telephone" medieval castle a 35 mile desert highway that "you can fry an egg on (...) at noon" journey away from any civilization to explain, then the second half, in which there's a lot of sneaking around in the dark with candlelight, and characters inevitably don the knights armor we saw earlier as cover, is simpler and slighter and apt to give the viewer the sense of "been there, done that". Like the face of Paul Manderley, whose right side features are completed concealed by the bandana mask, the film is very much of two halves: one half intriguing and very peculiar, the other half humdrum and rather familiar. And if the first half seems intricately constructed, then the second half feels rather tossed off. Once Retling and Hartford's scam is uncovered, and the film shifts gears with its first real murder, that of Hartford, and the revelation that the killer, Lucy's stepbrother Cesare, is somewhere in the castle, it becomes a more routine romp of a killer on the loose and everyone running around the castle.

But there's still the mystery of just what Manderley is hiding behind that face mask (even his own personal physician doesn't know). Earlier, Lucy was at pains to point out that Cesare Borgia was merely her *step*brother, with "no right to the (Borgia) name", but we know that the elusive Cesare carries a scar on the right side of his face, and there is a moment, as the suspicious Chan reaches for Manderley's face mask, where you think that just maybe the unmentionable may be true, but when Chan rips the mask off from Manderley's face, he of course reveals... exactly what you would expect to be there.

This would be fated to be the last of the Charlie Chan films from Twentieth Century-Fox, the studio shutting down its B-picture unit and scaling back its film production upon the United States' entry into World War II. And it's as if the filmmakers knew the end was near and decided to throw in everything they had, but at the same time didn't have a lot left in the tank. The result is something that is strange, yet usual; eccentric, yet conventional; off the wall, yet by the numbers.

We're a long way away from CHARLIE CHAN IN LONDON now, with a story that takes place not on other side of the planet, but figuratively and literally just down the road, and with the car's distributor then removed just to make absolutely sure that the adventure can go no further. In my commentary on Warner Oland's final film, CHARLIE CHAN AT MONTE CARLO, I remarked that the noisy, spluttering, broken down, go-nowhere taxi hailed for Chan and Lee in that film was an apt metaphor for the picture itself, and so to is the regal looking sedan that transports Chan and King to Manderley Castle in CASTLE IN THE DESERT symbolic of its film; making half of its journey with style and grandeur, before being found to have something vital missing.

If you're one who likes to follow the plot and try to deduce the killer, you may cry foul in protest as plot hole after plot hole abounds, while those more willing to just go along for the ride will giggle and gurgle with glee as absurdity is compounded upon absurdity. Like that other Lachman-Larkin collaboration, DEAD MEN TELL, CASTLE IN THE DESERT is less logical and literal in its storytelling than other Chan films are (why do scammers invite the world's foremost detective to witness their scamming?), instead going for mood and atmosphere and thematic richness: The crisp, stylish visuals, the lighting, the camera angles, and the sheer volume of props on display, makes each set loaded with detail and each frame beautifully crafted. Then there are the wonderfully eccentric characterizations (including Ethel Griffies and Milton Parsons, who both also had memorable roles in DEAD MEN TELL), and the rich medieval castle setting, with its candle chandeliers and torture dudgeon and poison rack. But while the content the these trappings surrounds - the Manderleys issues and the scammers' plot - is interesting, it's not captivating or satisfying in the way that, say, Captain Kane's tale of obsession and revenge in DEAD MEN TELL was, and nor does this film, for all its similarities, quite match that one.

Ultimately, this moody, bizarre, ultra-stylish, dreamlike film is liable to be either one of your absolute favorites or one of your absolute least. But however one feels about CASTLE IN THE DESERT, one can't deny that the series went out in style.

BEST MOMENT: [11:14] - Chan, dabbing his perspiring face with a handkerchief, sits beneath the scorching sun on the steps of the Mojave Wells Hotel while he waits for his ride to Manderley Castle, having been exiled from the shade of the hotel's porch by the hotel owner, whose attitude toward Chan plummets from ingratiatingly hospitable to downright hostile with naught in between upon learning the reason for Chan's visit to the town. "We don't want nobody who does business with the castle" he says, still reeling from having Gleeson's dead body dumped on him (huh?) and keen to disassociate himself from any future ill fortune the castle may bring.

The local fortune teller, Madame Saturnia, exiting her store across the street, spots Chan and makes a beeline for him. She brings a message from stars, and though she speaks her words with clarity and certainty, Chan is not to be deterred, and cheerily fends off her ominous words of warning, countering them with his wise philosophies:

Saturnia: You have enemies, Mr. Chan.
Chan: Man without enemies like dog without fleas.
Saturnia: I see death reaching for you, like an arrow.
Chan: Desert without Indians very safe.
Saturnia: Leave the desert. Death waits for you out there. Go back where you came from, unless you're prepared to die.
Chan: Man who fears death die thousand times.

Saturnia shrugs. She's done her part, delivered her notice. Whatever happens now will happen, and Chan can't say she didn't warn him (Chan will later be heard to remark that "sharp wit sometimes much better than deadly weapon". If true then he is at least well armed). On his head be it.

Just then the car bearing the crest of the Borgias arrives. Watson King, who has just checked out of the hotel, appears, and he too, as the hotel owner is aghast to learn, is bound for Manderley Castle. Chan and King present their invitations to the chauffeur and climb into the car.

As the car drives off into the desert, Saturnia approaches the hotel manager, curious as to the identity of the second person. "He'll die a violent death, he will" she says with certainty, as if stating an unavoidable fact. "And his murderer shall go unpunished".

IN SHORT: The Twentieth Century-Fox *Charlie Chan* series draws to a close with this bizarre, dreamlike entry. Low on logic, high on production niceties.

Of Truth and Justice: Oland vs. Toler

"Truth like football, receive many kicks before reaching goal"
-Charlie Chan, CHARLIE CHAN AT THE OLYMPICS

"Justice can be brought to dead men"
-Charlie Chan, CHARLIE CHAN AT THE WAX MUSEUM

Ah. *The* question. Oland or Toler? Most likely you should enjoy both Chans. Both were very good and both proved well suited to the role, the series very fortunate to have struck gold not once, but twice. And yet, it's also likely that you'll prefer one over the other, even if just a little. Perhaps it's the one you saw first, who you consider "your" Charlie Chan, or maybe it's simply that one portrayal appeals to you or resonates with you a little more than the other.

OlandChan has a sincerity about him that shines through with every word he utters, a kindness and warmth that radiates whenever he offers others comfort and reassurance. He's sometimes giddy, sometimes dour, sometimes a seemingly docile and rotund figure, fiddling with his hat or holding it out in front of him with his fingertips, but there's also a fire that burns behind the eyes, that can be seen whenever he faces a killer or is suspicious of someone's words or actions. Watch how his eyes positively bore into the squirming Fred Gage in CHARLIE CHAN'S SECRET, when Gage arrives shortly after an attempt is made on Chan's life. It's a different kind of intimidating, one silent but potent. Toler doesn't have that.

TolerChan, on the other hand, is more ironic, his glances more overtly cunning and shrewd. In his first three outings he's more animated (see CHARLIE CHAN IN HONOLULU, when he gets news that he's become a grandfather, or CHARLIE CHAN IN RENO, as he and Curtis Whitman rush to Mary's aid), and apt to give that big smile. In subsequent films this would be smoothed out as his characterization became more dignified and more regal (and perhaps more monotone). But what is very evident right from the beginning is his intelligence and wry guile. Sometimes it almost feels like he knew the answer all along, and was just waiting for the right time to pull the curtain string. There's also a sense that Toler's Chan enjoys and maybe even revels in his work, as opposed to Oland's more reluctant champion, whose natural detective abilities are, not exactly a burden or cross to bear, but certainly business rather than pleasure. There's the way TolerChan toys with his uncomfortable suspects, like a cat playing with a mouse he's just caught by the tail. Oland doesn't have that.

But Oland's Chan manages to feel more personally involved and emotionally invested in the drama and the goings on, more a part of things (except for in his last two, which don't really count), while also maintaining that level of profound detachment. Conversely, Toler's Chan is more external to the drama and happenings, and while he's perhaps more worldly, he's somehow less "*other* worldly". And while both are, of course, apt to wax philosophical and wise via Chan's famous aphorisms, Toler's Chanisms feel from the head, while Oland's Chanisms feel from the heart, with TolerChan's clever asides springing forth from his wit and intelligence, and OlandChan's profound reflections being drawn from personal life experience and deep contemplation.

Then there are the types of investigations that they participate in. OlandChan stories tend to be more forensic and clue based, with a focus on the evidence and on putting together the puzzles. See CHARLIE CHAN AT THE CIRCUS or CHARLIE CHAN AT THE RACE TRACK in particular, or any passage where Chan gives a walkthrough of the physical evidence of the murder scene or demonstrates the mechanics of something, such as the violin in CHARLIE CHAN IN EYGPT or the window latch in CHARLIE CHAN IN SHANGHAI, working out where everything goes and what everything means, disproving the base assumptions of others and getting to the truth of what really happened. There's a great clarity and certainty to the way that OlandChan explains things (see the timecard stamps in CHARLIE CHAN AT THE OLYMPICS for a particularly good example). Of course, OlandChan was quite capable when it came to questioning witnesses too, with a wonderful way of hinting to a suspect that he knows that they know more than they let on. "Very strange", he might begin after having been shown something or told something, not entirely on the level, "am sure that...", but, in CHARLIE CHAN AT THE CIRCUS, for example, he has little interaction with the principle suspects until late in the film, spending far more time with Tim and Tiny, the innocent circus midgets caught up in the drama.

Conversely, TolerChan mysteries are apt to be more testimony and interrogation based, with a focus on the suspects, who are generally a more colorful and eccentric assortment than the somewhat more non-descript beings who tended to inhabit the Oland's stories. CHARLIE CHAN IN RENO, CHARLIE CHAN IN PANAMA and DEAD MEN TELL in particular are all about the suspects, the characters. See also the intelligent thrusts and parries between Chan and Dr. Cardigan in CHARLIE CHAN IN HONOLULU, or Chan's physiological profiling of Dr. Zodiac in CHARLIE CHAN AT TREASURE ISLAND. That said, Toler could always deliver a crisp, clear summation too, holding his hands out in front of him as if he were drawing in all the pieces of the puzzle and directing them to their proper place, like a conductor of an orchestra. But while Toler's films brought the rouges and the red herrings to the forefront, they often pushed the innocents and the "lovers in peril" and the personal drama aspect of the stories into the background.

The films of both tenures, of course, are on the whole very much concocted from the same Charlie Chan formula, and have plenty of both physical evidence and suspect questioning, but TolerChan's scenes regarding the clues left behind at the murder scene are fewer and shorter and don't seem as involving (see CHARLIE CHAN'S MURDER CRUISE's rather unengaging items of "interest"). CHARLIE CHAN RENO, Toler's second film, does has a lot of poking about the murder scene, but the denouement, where characters are required to don the same clothes that they wore on the night of murder, somehow isn't as strong as, say, the similar finale of Oland's THE BLACK CAMEL where the characters assumed the same seating positions as the evening before.

Finally, there's the matter of Chan's role, his principle driving purpose, as the protagonist of the stories. Obviously, in all of the films, no matter the lead actor, Chan's prime objective is to solve the mystery and unmask killer, sifting though several suspects and putting together the clues, while avoiding occasional attempts on his life. But there were recurring differences in the way Chan's motivation for doing so was positioned and played out depending on the actor.

OlandChan's motives are quite often more based on keeping innocent people out of jail, or getting innocent people who are in trouble out of trouble, and it just so happens that the best way to do this is to find the killer. In CHARLIE CHAN IN LONDON, Chan notes that if the condemned Paul Gray is really innocent, then some other person must have committed the murder, and that the "only method to save Mr. Gray is to find this other. Quick", while in CHARLIE CHAN AT THE CIRCUS he joins the investigation because it's the only way to prevent the circus from "going to pieces". OlandChan is often initially not even interested in taking on the case until the human face is put on it. See CHARLIE CHAN IN LONDON, when he picks up Pamela's engagement ring from the floor, or CHARLIE CHAN AT THE CIRCUS, where it's his children who plead with him not to let the circus be shut down (the few Oland films that that don't have this element, such as CHARLIE CHAN AT MONTE CARLO, seem to lack a sense of purpose). And generally in the Oland films, a party has already been earmarked for the murder by the local authorities prior to Chan's arrival - again think Paul Gray in CHARLIE CHAN IN LONDON, or Yvette Lamartine in CHARLIE CHAN IN PARIS, or Gravelle in CHARLIE CHAN AT THE OPERA, or, for a few moments at least, Test Pilot Edwards in CHARLIE CHAN AT THE OLYMPICS - and it's up to Chan to get these hasty verdicts overturned, by getting to the truth.

TolerChan, however, tends to be more focused on apprehending the killer, locking guilty people away. Two films have him hunting down notorious saboteurs (CHARLIE CHAN IN PANAMA, MURDER OVER NEW YORK), and another two serial killers (CHARLIE CHAN'S MURDER CRUISE, CASTLE IN THE DESERT). True, in Toler's CHARLIE CHAN IN RENO, an early exception, Chan's involvement in the investigation is launched by his desire to aid the falsely accused Mary Whitman, but once he arrives she is very quickly exonerated, and this aspect of the story is more or less dropped from the rest of the film. More often, the murder victim is an old friend and/or a fellow investigator (think Inspector Duff in CHARLIE CHAN'S MURDER CRUISE - *"vicious attack in own office bitter challenge to friendship. Challenge will not go unanswered"*), or someone who we get to know quite well in short time before they are slain, and now it is a matter of meting out justice.

Oland's Chan as an instrument of truth, Toler's Chan as an instrument of justice? Of course, the two aren't mutually exclusive and go together, the above generalization simultaneously broad and slight and not without its exceptions. But in the Oland films, it's the people caught up in the fallout from the murder with whom we are intended to sympathize, while in the Toler films, it's more often that not the murdered themselves (in the Oland films, we sometimes barely meet the victim at all).

It's also worth nothing that in the Oland films, the murder is usually a one-off on the part of the killer (later attempts on Chan's life for sticking his nose in notwithstanding), a means and an end. The killer has generally killed everyone that they intend to kill, and inflicted all the damage that they intend to inflict, before Chan has arrived on the scene, and Chan is dealing with the fallout and aiding those caught in the confusion. But in the Toler films, where the murder is usually merely a beginning, one sin in a much larger plot, it's often the case that the killer will go on to kill more people and do more damage unless they are stopped.

In either case, it's our favorite detective Charlie Chan applying his skills and intelligence to solve a murder mystery, ensuring that justice is served and seeing that the truth is brought to life (while dropping a few of his Chanisms along the way), but if you do prefer one Chan over the other, all this might go part of the way to explaining why.

So if the Oland films are **truth**, and the Toler films at Fox are **justice**, does that make the *Charlie Chan* films made at Monogram Pictures, with Chan now working for the U.S. Government, **the American way**?

TO BE CONTINUED

CHARLIE CHAN AT TWENTIETH CENTURY-FOX

1   CHARLIE CHAN CARRIES ON (1931)*
2   THE BLACK CAMEL (1931)
3   CHARLIE CHAN'S CHANCE (1932)*
4   CHARLIE CHAN'S GREATEST CASE (1933)*
5   CHARLIE CHAN'S COURAGE (1934)*
6   CHARLIE CHAN IN LONDON (1934)
7   CHARLIE CHAN IN PARIS (1935)
8   CHARLIE CHAN IN EGYPT (1935)
9   CHARLIE CHAN IN SHANGHAI (1935)
10   CHARLIE CHAN'S SECRET (1936)
11   CHARLIE CHAN AT THE CIRCUS (1936)
12   CHARLIE CHAN AT THE RACE TRACK (1936)
13   CHARLIE CHAN AT THE OPERA (1936)
14   CHARLIE CHAN AT THE OLYMPICS (1937)
15   CHARLIE CHAN ON BROADWAY (1937)
16   CHARLIE CHAN AT MONTE CARLO (1937)
17   CHARLIE CHAN IN HONOLULU (1938)
18   CHARLIE CHAN IN RENO (1938)
19   CHARLIE CHAN AT TREASURE ISLAND (1939)
20   CHARLIE CHAN IN CITY IN DARKNESS (1939)
21   CHARLIE CHAN IN PANAMA (1940)
22   CHARLIE CHAN'S MURDER CRUISE (1940)
23   CHARLIE CHAN AT THE WAX MUSEUM (1940)
24   MURDER OVER NEW YORK (1940)
25   DEAD MEN TELL (1941)
26   CHARLIE CHAN IN RIO (1941)
27   CASTLE IN THE DESERT (1942)

* - Lost film

About the Author

LUKE FREEMAN was born in 1982. He resides in Melbourne, Australia. *The Charlie Chan Mystery Movie Guide* is his first book.

CPSIA information can be obtained at www.ICGtesting.com
Printed in the USA
BVOW09s2334081014

370065BV00027B/530/P

9 780992 561901